PERSPECTIVES ON WRITING
Series Editors, Susan H. McLeod and Rich Rice

PERSPECTIVES ON WRITING
Series Editors, Susan H. McLeod and Rich Rice

The Perspectives on Writing series addresses writing studies in a broad sense. Consistent with the wide ranging approaches characteristic of teaching and scholarship in writing across the curriculum, the series presents works that take divergent perspectives on working as a writer, teaching writing, administering writing programs, and studying writing in its various forms.

The WAC Clearinghouse and Parlor Press are collaborating so that these books will be widely available through free digital distribution and low-cost print editions. The publishers and the Series editor are teachers and researchers of writing, committed to the principle that knowledge should freely circulate. We see the opportunities that new technologies have for further democratizing knowledge. And we see that to share the power of writing is to share the means for all to articulate their needs, interest, and learning into the great experiment of literacy.

Recent Books in the Series

Nathan Shepley, *Placing the History of College Writing: Stories from the Incomplete Archive* (2015)

Asao B. Inoue, *Antiracist Writing Assessment Ecologies: An Approach to Teaching and Assessing Writing for a Socially Just Future* (2015)

Theresa Lillis, Kathy Harrington, Mary R. Lea, and Sally Mitchell (Eds.), *Working with Academic Literacies: Case Studies Towards Transformative Practice* (2015)

Beth L. Hewett and Kevin Eric DePew (Eds.), *Foundational Practices of Online Writing Instruction* (2015)

Christy I. Wenger, *Yoga Minds, Writing Bodies: Contemplative Writing Pedagogy* (2015)

Sarah Allen, *Beyond Argument: Essaying as a Practice of (Ex)Change* (2015)

Steven J. Corbett, *Beyond Dichotomy: Synergizing Writing Center and Classroom Pedagogies* (2015)

Tara Roeder and Roseanne Gatto (Eds.), *Critical Expressivism: Theory and Practice in the Composition Classroom* (2014)

Terry Myers Zawacki and Michelle Cox (Eds), *WAC and Second-Language Writers: Research Towards Linguistically and Culturally Inclusive Programs and Practices*, (2014)

WAC PARTNERSHIPS BETWEEN SECONDARY AND POSTSECONDARY INSTITUTIONS

Edited by Jacob S. Blumner and Pamela B. Childers

The WAC Clearinghouse
wac.colostate.edu
Fort Collins, Colorado

Parlor Press
www.parlorpress.com
Anderson, South Carolina

The WAC Clearinghouse, Fort Collins, Colorado 80523-1052

Parlor Press, 3015 Brackenberry Drive, Anderson, South Carolina 29621

© 2016 by Jacob S. Blumner and Pamela B. Childers. This work is licensed under a Creative Commons Attribution-NonCommercial-NoDerivatives 4.0 International.

Printed in the United States of America

Library of Congress Cataloging-in-Publication Data

Names: Blumner, Jacob S., 1968- editor. | Childers, Pamela B., 1943- editor.
Title: WAC partnerships between secondary and postsecondary institutions / edited by Jacob S. Blumner and Pamela B. Childers.
Description: Fort Collins, Colorado : Parlor Press, [2016] | Series: Perspectives on writing | Includes bibliographical references.
Identifiers: LCCN 2016001106 (print) | LCCN 2016007275 (ebook) | ISBN 9781602358072 (pbk. : alk. paper) | ISBN 9781602358089 (hardcover : alk. paper) | ISBN 9781602358096 (pdf) | ISBN 9781602358102 (epub) | ISBN 9781602358119 (iBook) | ISBN 9781602358126 (mobi)
Subjects: LCSH: English language--Composition and exercises--Study and teaching (Secondary) | Interdisciplinary approach in education. | College-school cooperation.
Classification: LCC LB1631 .W2 2016 (print) | LCC LB1631 (ebook) | DDC 808/.0420712--dc23
LC record available at http://lccn.loc.gov/2016001106

Copyeditor: Don Donahue
Designer: Mike Palmquist
Series Editors: Susan H. McLeod and Rich Rice

Cover Image: "Serenade in a Kansas Wind," Wax Pencil Drawing by Malcolm Graeme Childers. Copyright © 1998 by Malcolm Childers. Used with permission.
Poem: "Serenade in a Kansas Wind," page 3, ©1998 Malcolm Graeme Childers.

This book is printed on acid-free paper.

The WAC Clearinghouse supports teachers of writing across the disciplines. Hosted by Colorado State University, it brings together scholarly journals and book series as well as resources for teachers who use writing in their courses. This book is available in digital format for free download at http://wac.colostate.edu.

Parlor Press, LLC is an independent publisher of scholarly and trade titles in print and multimedia formats. This book is available in print and digital formats from Parlor Press at http://www.parlorpress.com. For submission information or to find out about Parlor Press publications, write to Parlor Press, 3015 Brackenberry Drive, Anderson, South Carolina 29621, or email editor@parlorpress.com.

CONTENTS

Foreword vii
    Art Young

Acknowledgments xi

Serenade in a Kansas Wind 3
    Malcolm Childers

Chapter 1. Introduction to WAC and Partnerships That Cross Academic Levels and Disciplines 5
    Jacob S. Blumner and Pamela B. Childers

Chapter 2. Talking about Writing Across the Secondary and College Community 19
    Michelle Cox and Phyllis Gimbel

Chapter 3. Newton's Third Law Revisited: Action Reaction Pairs in Collaboration 37
    Michael J. Lowry

Chapter 4. Shaping Disciplinary Discourses in High School: A Two-Way Collaborative Writing Program 47
    Federico Navarro and Andrea Revel Chion

Chapter 5. Collaborating on Writing-to-Learn in Ninth-Grade Science: What Is Collaboration—and How Can We Sustain It? 63
    Danielle Myelle-Watson, Deb Spears, David Wellen, Michael McClellan, and Brad Peters

Chapter 6. In Our Own Backyard: What Makes a Community College-Secondary School Connection Work? 87
    Mary McMullen-Light

Chapter 7. Negotiating Expectations: Overcoming Obstacles Introducing WAC through Collaboration between a German University Writing Center and German High Schools 113
    Luise Beaumont, Mandy Pydde, and Simone Tschirpke

Chapter 8. "So Much More Than Just an 'A'": A Transformative High School and University Writing Center Partnership 131
    Marie Hansen, Debra Hartley, Kirsten Jamsen, Katie Levin, and Kristen Nichols-Besel

**Chapter 9. "Oh, I Get By with a Little Help from My Friends":
Short-Term Writing Center/Community Collaborations 155**
    Trixie G. Smith

**Chapter 10. What We Have Learned about WAC Partnerships
and Their Futures 167**
    Jacob S. Blumner and Pamela B. Childers

Contributors..175

FOREWORD

Art Young
Clemson University

Since the 1970s, Writing Across the Curriculum (WAC) has been an educational movement devoted to students of all ages learning disciplinary content as they simultaneously develop their language abilities. Elementary schools, secondary schools, and colleges all experimented with a variety of approaches to WAC, and since the 1980s, WAC has been a significant presence in American education at all levels as teachers seek to make connections between students' writing and their learning of subject matter—within the broader framework of increasing students' critical-thinking, problem-solving, and creative abilities. A motivated and engaged writer and learner is a successful student no matter the disciplinary knowledge being learned.

A major premise of WAC is that subject-matter teachers and writing teachers should work together "across disciplines" to make WAC approaches to disciplinary writing and learning more effective and meaningful. Whether in physics classes or in writing classes, when teachers work in isolation the result often is a rote-learning approach rather than an active-learning approach. WAC, on the other hand, demonstrates that partnering with other teachers will improve student learning and communication abilities.

WAC Partnerships between Secondary and Post-Secondary Institutions builds on traditional approaches to WAC based on the collaboration of teachers from different disciplines, collaborations often initiated by an interdisciplinary faculty workshop—what one of the authors in this collection refers to as "the quintessential WAC experience." But this book goes further and proposes that teachers and institutions partner not only across disciplines in their schools and colleges, but also across educational levels and with other community organizations—locally, regionally, nationally, and even internationally. Two of the chapters are by teacher-researchers in Argentina and in Germany. The editors and authors in *WAC Partnerships* envision exciting possibilities for teachers, students, and institutions that embrace WAC, an educational movement begun over 45 years ago, but now in the twenty-first century more than ever full of opportunities and possibilities.

My involvement with WAC began in the 1970s and early 1980s, exciting times for educational initiatives. My colleagues and I at Michigan Technological University developed interdisciplinary workshops and cross-disciplinary projects in which teachers at opposite ends of the campus came together to develop strategies for improving students' writing abilities and subject-matter knowledge through a variety of teacher-to-teacher projects and department-to-department projects. We conducted workshops in local elementary and secondary schools, and we partnered on workshops with institutions in other states. We started a writing center with tutors who replaced decontextualized self-paced, fill-in-the-blanks, learning modules. My colleague Toby Fulwiler founded and co-directed the Upper Peninsula Writing Project (UPWP), an affiliate of the National Writing Project (NWP). UPWP soon had an emphasis on WAC, inviting teachers from disciplines other than English to enroll, as well as maintaining NWP's principles of emphasizing writing process theory and pedagogy and a teachers-as-writers approach to building and expressing knowledge. But, as you will read in this book, these activities are just the beginning of opportunities that now await engaged teachers and institutions that form partnerships across disciplines and across educational levels.

Jacob S. Blumner and Pamela B. Childers, nationally-known and respected teacher-researchers on WAC and writing centers at both the secondary and post-secondary levels, have collected and edited an engaging and important anthology that will be of special interest to teachers and administrators already participating in or seeking to participate in WAC and writing center programs and possibilities. *WAC Partnerships* provides models for collaborations between secondary and higher education institutions and between individual teachers in different educational settings. Readers learn of a successful collaboration between a private high school and a public community college that provides an example of best practices when planning to build a partnership. Readers also learn of a partnership between a high school and a university that was not successful, offering a case study in mistakes that may lead to failure. Readers learn of collaboration between a high school writing center and a university writing center that creates substantial and unexpected benefits for the student tutors in both locations.

These partnerships and others in this volume are presented in the context of new opportunities for WAC and writing centers brought about by recent changes in local, national, and global educational cultures, from new technologies that support collaboration across distances, and educational policies designed to equip students to contribute and even thrive in the information-driven world of the twenty-first century. Such opportunities emerge from new educational policies, such as the Common Core State Standards for writing and literacy, to prepare students for writing in college, a key area for partnerships between secondary schools and colleges, and from STEM, a curricular innovation in science, technology, engineering, and math, which focuses on writing in the science and engineering disciplines in high school and college. One essay by a high school science teacher reports on a collaboration between NASA senior scientists and secondary science teachers who are dedicated to "supporting the next generation of STEM professionals." Key components of this collaboration are the use of WAC strategies, such as problem-based learning, frequent informal writing-to-learn activities, and formal writing-to-communicate assignments and projects for both teachers and students.

Other fresh opportunities for WAC and writing centers are being created every day by the rapid development of digital communication technologies, technologies that allow students, teachers, and institutions to collaborate across short and long distances on both short and long term projects. Electronic communication tools such as email, blogs, Skype, and other social media provide numerous resources for WAC programs and writing centers and the individual students, teachers, tutors, and clients within them to develop individual and institutional partnerships to enhance students' engagement and learning. One essay by a writing center director describes a short-term project in which writing center consultants in training at her university in the US partner with new consultants in training at a university in Sweden through email discussions about recent tutoring experiences and shared readings.

I can attest that such direct personal conversations using electronic communication with distant partners can be extremely rewarding for students and teachers, sharpening through conversational learning participants' reading and writing abilities, subject-matter knowledge, and critical thinking. At Clemson University since 1987, I have seen remarkable engagement and thoughtful and insightful learning when my students in South Carolina discussed William Blake's poetry via email exchange with students in Andreas Pellizzari's English class at Alessandro Volta High School in Bagno a Ripoli, Italy, and when my students discussed Tim O'Brien's novel *The Things They Carried* on a blog with students in Nancy Swanson's creative writing class at Daniel High School in Central, South Carolina, just five miles from Clemson. In both cases, the often great distance between high school teachers and students and college teachers and students was bridged, making these writing-across-the-literature-curriculum projects successful as participants used their language abilities to build knowledge and perspectives not available to any one individual. In a longer term project, 2003-2013, students in English classes each year at Clemson University have discussed various American, British, and Swedish poets on blogs with engineering and science students in Magnus Gustafsson's "Fiction for Engineers" classes at Chalmers University in Gothenburg, Sweden. Students were quick to discover the cultural and linguistic differences in the critical interpretations of Swedish students compared to American students, a multi-cultural collaboration not available before the advent of rapid, asynchronous, international communication.

I am pleased to offer this foreword to *WAC Partnerships between Secondary and Post-Secondary Institutions,* which describes valuable current models for planning, building, and maintaining partnerships between institutions, as well as sound advice from experienced practitioners for teachers and students seeking to extend the boundaries of their learning through collaboration in WAC and writing center projects.

WAC Partnerships shows that engineers and scientists are excited to support "the next generation of STEM professionals." No matter our disciplines, we teachers strive to strengthen the abilities of all our students as they prepare for their professional and civic lives. In particular, teachers involved in WAC and writing centers recognize that students who become more able learners and communicators, some of whom are our junior colleagues as consultants in writing centers and teaching fellows in WAC programs, will one day be strengthening the language and learning abilities of the students they teach, counsel, and serve.

ACKNOWLEDGMENTS

It is hard to acknowledge all of the people who have influenced our professional work, writing, and thinking over the years. Jacob began considering the role of WAC and writing centers while he was studying and presenting with colleagues at University of Nevada-Reno in 1993. Pam started her study of WAC and writing centers by partnering with other secondary school and university people in 1981 through Northeastern University. However, we began collaborating at the 1997 IWCA conference in Park City, UT, while Jacob and Bob Barnett were editing *Writing Centers and Writing Across the Curriculum Programs: Building Interdisciplinary Partnerships*. Pam was writing a chapter for the book, and we met in the makeshift writing center in the lobby of the conference hotel to work on her revisions. So, over the years we have had the opportunity to work with a variety of people in multiple settings who have influenced our belief in the importance of partnerships among secondary schools, community colleges, and four-year institutions.

We wish to acknowledge all of those who have shared their experiences with partnerships and ideas from their own research and presentations at conferences, questioned what we were doing, attended workshops and presentations we have given, and supported what we have attempted to do through many missteps and revisions. We also wish to voice our appreciation to our students in diverse settings who inspire us and teach us.

Sometimes we overlook the obvious; it is the volunteer professional organizations that have enabled us to continue to do what we love and come in contact with one another—NCTE, IWAC, IWCA, CCCC, as well as all the state and regional groups. We have met or learned about our authors in this collection through these connections, and they have made us intellectually richer in the process. We would also like to thank our home institutions that have allowed us to pursue our research interests and supported our work. And we would like to thank Nancy Grigg for her editing prowess helping whip the book into shape, and Malcolm Childers for his vision that became our cover drawing and his poem, "Serenade in a Kansas Wind."

Outside of our professional work, we must acknowledge and thank our families for their support. Their encouragement, patience, and understanding make the work possible. Jacob first and foremost thanks his wife, Helen, who has been the rock of the family, supporting Jacob as he burned the midnight oil on this project. He also wants to thank his three sons, Jonas, Micah, and Eli for inspiring this work and making it more meaningful. And finally he thanks his whole family for dragging him outside to ride a bike or go fishing when they know he needs fresh air and to feel unfiltered sunlight. Pam thanks her husband Malcolm for his love, support, and partnership on writing projects and presentations, as well as in life. She also wishes to thank her parents for their love and work ethic, her family and friends who challenge her thinking and actions daily, and her former students from whom she continues to learn. Pam's work with Mesa Land Trust has given her an opportunity to help conserve our environment and its riches for future generations.

Finally, we wish to thank Sue McLeod and Mike Palmquist for their support throughout this project. The *WAC Clearinghouse*, an international storehouse of professional volunteerism, offers everyone open-access materials, journals and books. What a gift to our profession.

WAC PARTNERSHIPS BETWEEN SECONDARY AND POSTSECONDARY INSTITUTIONS

SERENADE IN A KANSAS WIND

Malcolm Childers

Stand
just here,
in such a way
that the sweeping
copper lines converge--
an ever-shrinking
prophetic mirage
in both directions
toward the horizon.

Now
close your eyes
and lean your head back,
so that the sun can wash
your salty brow.

In the amber half light
behind your lids,
your thoughts will focus
on what your mind can see
and
something of the middle ground--
what it means to be in this place
where East becomes West--
will reach out
and touch you.

From the early
supple greens of spring,
this great grass ocean
begins to spill,
flow,
and flower in the wind.
During those living months,
birds and insects
dance and sing--
a primal buzzing,
twittering floor show
of sex,
predation,
and passing.

Like
a grand expeditionary force,
they spread a thousand miles north
from here
into Manitoba.

Then drying,
their life
begins to fall back
like a defeated army
clad in the the hissing
brittle yellow of autumn.
It retreats
a thousand miles
south from here
into Tamaulipas.

Maybe you can sense
there used to be
more.

Perhaps
you can just hear
the American Serengeti
that was.

The endless brown armadas
of large animals
plying the grass ocean,
the indigenous nomads
who moved with them,
who lived from them,
who knew great risk
and even greater freedom,
who danced and sang
their primal invocations
of sex,

predation,
and passing.

Perhaps
you can just hear
what it was like
before these wires
crossed the sky,
before the time
of white men,
before everything changed
to conform
to their European
God-given mandate
to subdue
and possess the earth.

Still
sometimes,
in the thin winter light,
long after the vacationers
have hurried through
without seeing,
without caring,
as if they had never been;
and only an occasional semi
reads the icy concrete pages
as it passes indifferently
from Dodge to Wichita,
the wires themselves
will sing.
And the sound of it.

How to describe
that sound.

It is
as if all
that has passed here in time
where we stand
listening
comes again
as a chorus of the ages.

Within
the penetrating hum
and breathy moan of it,
are the lowing of wild herds,
the intimate passion and birth cries
of native women,
the ceremonial chants
of their men,
the screech of wheeling hawks,
the last prayers of wounded settlers and
dying braves,
the raging curses of betrayal,
the brass of victory bands,
the hammering of builders,
the buzzing of back-room dealers,
the twittering of evening ladies,
the rhythmic songs of workmen,
the whistles and calls of cowboys,
the throaty din of tractors,
the quiet songs of farm wives,
and the lonely rumble
of distant trains passing through at
twilight.

Within the soft
and strident passages
of that longing sound
there are melodies
of a subtle and oceanic nature.
Within those lost chords
are intervals
that might
change the world
if we only could hear them.
If we only knew them.
But then
it's only you and I listening,
and the quite serenade rings
endlessly on
as if no one
will ever
answer the phone.

CHAPTER 1

INTRODUCTION TO WAC AND PARTNERSHIPS THAT CROSS ACADEMIC LEVELS AND DISCIPLINES

Jacob S. Blumner and Pamela B. Childers

Every day we read about the gap between high school and college writing, how high schools are not preparing students for college writing, and after all the handwringing and finger pointing, many teachers and scholars contend that high school-college partnerships would be the most effective way to solve this problem. As we wrote in "Building Better Bridges: What Makes High School-College WAC Collaborations Work?":

> To better prepare students for writing across the curriculum in higher education, some high school teachers and college professors have formed partnerships. The idea is that a cross-pollination of ideas from the teachers, who know the students best, and the professors, who know the expectations and forms of college writing best, could greatly benefit students, teachers, and professors. Why do some programs fail and others succeed? What in successful partnerships might be replicated by others? (Blumner and Childers 91)

Through our interactions with teachers at all academic levels involved in WAC partnerships, we discovered the need to demonstrate a variety of successful models with various collaborations between schools and institutions, so others can emulate them and use the book as a model to work with a variety of stakeholders in promoting this type of collaboration. Our research, done through our own scholarship, International Writing Across the Curriculum Conference workshops (2010 and 2012), and a survey that led to a publication (Blumner and Childers), provides a sound footing for this book as well as confirms the need for such literature. We present here a collection of collaborative partnerships among middle schools, high schools, colleges and universities to improve writing across the curriculum (WAC). Schools and colleges are forming partnerships to improve WAC and student matriculation as they have seen an increasing need for more coordinated efforts to prepare students for the kinds of work and civic engagement that is increasingly required of people to succeed and contribute to our society. The Common Core State Standards (CCSS) refer to this as college and career readiness.

Renée Clift, Mary Lou Veal, Marlene Johnson, and Patricia Holland define collaboration as "The explicit agreement among two or more persons to meet together over time to set and accomplish a particular goal or goals" (54). The purpose of this book is to promote models of collaborative partnerships across the curriculum and across schools/colleges, so other institutions can design their own programs or create new innovative ones. Also, we want to encourage sustainability in such partnerships based on what has and has not worked for others. These partnerships vary from secondary to postsecondary WAC partnerships, all involve WAC, and many include writing centers as part of the partnerships. Each chapter has been written by participants from the institutions at the core of that particular collaboration and detail their program and their experiences in it, addressing topics such as pedagogy, philosophy, budgeting, daily pragmatics, problems encountered, benefits, results and recommendations. Contributors include educators in South America and Germany who wish to share their partnership experiences as well. All authors have read and responded to other chapters, and readers will note how authors reference work from other chapters in their own to create a cohesive connection and model collaboration throughout the entire book. In fact, this book itself is an example of another kind of partnership, one in which there are no hierarchical differences among participants and no standard for what does and does not work. Our authors are unique educators who approach partnerships based on their own backgrounds, experiences, research, students, disciplines, institutions, and state or national standards. Our readers are also exceptional educators who will adapt what is included in these chapters to their own backgrounds, experiences, research, students, disciplines, institutions and state or national standards.

WHY PARTNERSHIPS? ADVANTAGES/DISADVANTAGES

Whether initiated by the secondary or postsecondary institution, the partnership has to be a highly collaborative one. As we noted in our brief introduction, authors frequently refer to the advantages for both partners involved. And, with knowledge of upcoming changes in the SAT, both secondary and postsecondary educators will need to know more about what and how their collaborative partners are teaching writing. For high school partners, there is an overwhelming need for some professional development to assist teachers in applying WAC theory into practice in all disciplines. Educators know their students and understand their potential, but sometimes lack the knowledge of how to use writing in all subjects to improve critical thinking, learning and writing. Through collaborative planning with colleagues, they can design ways that do not make more work for them, but instead help their students learn while they assess their own teaching as well. Administrators are limited in the amount of time and monetary assistance they can offer to such projects. In dual credit (DC) courses, "beginning these programs is typically less expensive and faster to start for the [high schools], since the (DC) approach does not require external workshops to operate, nor does it require an expensive and stressful test to validate the class" (Uhlenkamp). For instance, in Chapter 8 of this volume, the authors describe how the high school teacher had to offer assistance in her own classroom without any funds to do much more until she created a partnership with the nearby university and began a peer tutoring/coaching program through the partnership. We believe this experience is not uncommon. And, as we hear more and more about CCSS, partnerships can be an important advantage if there is what Annette D. Digby, Barbara C. Gartin, and Nikki L. Murdick refer to in "Developing Effective University and Public School Partnerships" as "communication, concern, compromise, and commitment" (37) on the part of all involved. Without these four essential components, they may be unsuccessful or never partner at all (38).

For postsecondary institutions, the advantages include recruitment of future students to the institution, an understanding of what students have learned and how they mature before entering their first-year courses, a laboratory partnership for secondary education majors, and new perspectives on teaching and learning. Also, the college has minimal direct expenses in terms of faculty salaries and facility costs; high school teachers instruct dual credit courses on high school campuses (Uhlenkamp). Many partnerships involve classroom research that postsecondary instructors can conduct with their secondary partners, sometimes a necessary component for college faculty participation. We both have observed misconceptions that both partners have had because of the lack of communication, so a better understanding of what and how teachers are teaching and young adults are learning becomes extremely valuable not only to postsecondary teachers in all disciplines, but also especially for teachers of writing and secondary education courses.

The disadvantages for all partners usually involve working out the problems of time and money to establish and maintain the partnership. Digby, Gartin, and Murdick point out that partners have to work on "the synchronization of both partners' schedules to allow times for meeting and other partnership activities" (38). Many have noted that institutional structures, rules, and responsibilities cause unanticipated conflicts that can be overcome if the lines of communication and commitments are there. For instance, at the University of Arkansas where a team partnered with a public school nearby, the "university partners wished to research cooperative learning in the middle school science classroom, but the time selected was at the end of the school year" (Digby, Gartin, and Murdick 38). The problems of dealing with the end-of-year requirements at the middle school would not have allowed for authentic research, so the middle school teachers suggested that the research be conducted at the beginning of the following school year. Therefore, the partnership was able to continue because all partners were involved and flexible enough to accommodate each partner's needs.

And, what happens when the funds run out? Are the institutions willing to continue the collaboration by sharing the financial burden of continuing it, or are individuals involved in the partnership able to apply for and successfully receive grants to continue it? If these collaborations are to succeed long term, they are dependent upon the impact on students at both institutions as well. According to Kenneth Bernstein, when preparing students for the AP test, he could:

> not simultaneously prepare them to do well on [the essay] portion of the test and teach them to write in a fashion that would properly serve them at higher levels of education.... Now you are seeing the results in the students arriving at your institutions. They may be very bright. But we have not been able to prepare them for the kind of intellectual work that you [college instructors] have every right to expect of them. (32)

Kathryn Noble McDaniel, a university history professor, writes in "Read Long and Prosper: Five Do's and Don'ts for Preparing Students for College," that her college students are frequently required to complete thesis-length projects, but with "no preparation in writing longer papers, students become overwhelmed by the assignment. They do not know how to formulate a topic that can be explored in more than two or three pages" (85). She concludes that because of a lack of such experience, they also "lack confidence that they can write at length and in depth and that there is even anything worth saying beyond page two" (85). Both of these examples indicate why communication between secondary and postsecondary teachers could make a difference in the learning of all students and better prepare them for future writing, thinking, and learning experiences. It is more than just "transitioning" or bridging the gap. Also, notice that Bernstein is talking about dealing with test preparation rather than preparation for the intellectual experience of college, and he is frustrated by his situation, while McDaniel's frustration is dealing with students that teachers like Bernstein have had to send to her. Imagine a different scenario, like ones in many of our chapters, where these two educators meet and discuss goals that would eliminate both of their frustrations and help their students become more fulfilled writers and learners as they transition from secondary to postsecondary institutions of learning.

The challenges Digby, Gartin, and Murdick describe at University of Arkansas presuppose a philosophical and pedagogical alignment between secondary and post-secondary educators; yet we have seen relationships in which that is not the case. Though all educators have their students' success at the forefront, what that looks like and how it is achieved may differ markedly, as well as how requirements and pressure placed on educators may vary dramatically. Also, negotiating and understanding different participant and institutional cultures and roles in the partnership can strain relations between institutions. These presuppositions, requirements, and pressures can make aligning work between secondary and postsecondary education daunting, labor and time-intensive, and often uncompensated. The time it takes to create and maintain these collaborations can be exhausting and frustrating, and institutions may not value the work in meaningful ways that reward the educators involved, rather than simply adding their efforts to an already heavy workload.

Secondary and postsecondary partnerships can make a big difference to students, especially if they are actively involved in the collaborations. In describing how the Tar River Writing Project (TRWP) partnered with a local high school (Pitts County School District, NC) to redesign its graduation project, Stephanie West-Puckett and William P. Banks explain how "teachers, like any group of professionals both want and need to have some degree of agency in the construction of the curriculum that they teach ... Likewise ... students benefit from being involved in the creation of a new curriculum" (355). The principal and leaders of J. H. Rose High School had wanted "a curriculum that provides rich literacy instruction with embedded opportunities to read, write, speak, and listen in both virtual and face-to-face environments" (357). With this team of collaborators focusing on the same goals, the students will definitely benefit from this collaboration. In another collaboration between Boise State and a nearby public school, Rachel Bear, Heidi Estrem, James E. Fredricksen, and Dawn Shepherd state, "Our goal is to consider how our pedagogical decisions in these two different contexts might helpfully echo each other, providing opportunities for richer professional conversations and continued productive learning for students" (131). They conclude their chapter by saying that their high school and college educators "want our students to make contributions, to feel and to provide support for one another, to learn from more experienced writers, to write about topics and in different modes and media that matter to them and to others, and to feel connected to other members of the classroom community" (135).

We as educators should not be working in isolation. Educational changes have been encouraged through many partnerships. For instance, Digby, Gartin, and Murdick discovered, "The partners must be committed to the idea that forming a university/public school partnership will lead to improvement in the education system by increasing the quality of education for all involved" (38). In a similar way, Candyce Reynolds, Danielle D. Stevens, and Ellen West describe their cross-disciplinary study of student learning based on Malcolm Knowles' belief that "learning is facilitated when they [students] are confronted with a problem that needs to be solved and calls upon them to creatively address the problem" (53).

EDUCATIONAL MOVEMENTS AND PARTNERSHIPS

There are several educational movements that connect directly to high school-college partnerships. As an introduction to those not familiar with each of these educational movements, we will provide brief overviews with sources to help readers get a sense of the overlaps and discrepancies among these movements. For this chapter, we will be focusing on the CCSS in writing (http://www.corestandards.org/ELA-Literacy/CCRA/W) that notes students "develop the capacity to build knowledge on a subject through research projects and to respond analytically to literary and informational sources. To meet these goals, students must devote significant time and effort to writing, producing numerous pieces over short and extended time frames throughout the year." Some of our authors delve into more specific connections that promote healthy approaches to the CCSS without overwhelming secondary teachers with preparing students for an assessment. Michelle Cox and Phyllis Gimbel make these connections in "Conversations Among Teachers on Student Writing: WAC/Secondary Education Partnerships at BSU" in the special issue of *ATD* on *WAC in Secondary Schools* (http://wac.colostate.edu/atd/second_educ/cox_gimbel.cfm). Through partnerships with their postsecondary colleagues, teachers can connect the key concepts that students need to master in preparation for writing in college; and, these concepts are also essential to success with CCSS. For instance, the secondary and postsecondary educators in the Tar River Writing Project (TRWP) critically examined and questioned requirements of the CCSS in relation to the Framework for Success in Postsecondary Writing (http://wpacouncil.org/framework) and learned that "work with teachers around CCSS should move beyond comprehension of complex (and contradictory) texts and into collaborative critique, which creates opportunities for teachers to build capacity and excise agency in conversations about curriculum reform" (10).

Framework for Success in Postsecondary Writing (http://wpacouncil.org/framework) outlines expectations for incoming college students. The document describes eight habits of mind (curiosity, openness, engagement, creativity, persistence, responsibility, flexibility, and metacognition) and literacy-based skills and experiences (rhetorical knowledge, critical thinking, writing processes, knowledge of conventions, and the ability to compose in multiple environments). The Framework connects clearly to the principles of WAC. Authors of several chapters in this collection make these connections in describing how their partnerships encourage many of the concepts from the Framework. For instance, both Mary McMullen-Light (Chapter 6) and Marie Hansen et al. (Chapter 8) mention the importance of openness and critical thinking, while Trixie Smith (Chapter 9), McMullen-Light, and Hansen et al. discuss persistence and flexibility.

The newest version of Council of Writing Program Administrators Outcomes Statement for the First-Year Composition (http://wpacouncil.org/positions/outcomes.html), last amended in 2008, "describes the common knowledge, skills, and attitudes sought by first-year composition programs in American postsecondary education." Even though this statement specifically focuses on the first-year composition course, it serves as a guide for incoming first-year students in all disciplines; and, therefore, serves as a good place for partners at both academic levels to begin a dialogue. It is also written in an accessible and non-threatening way that can engage teachers and faculty from all subjects and disciplines. Because the Outcomes predate both Framework and CCSS, one can see the influence of them on both documents.

The goals of STEM education include encouraging educators to "invite our children to look at their school work as important to the world" (TIES). As Pamela B. Childers and Michael J. Lowry point out in referring to the *Atlas of Science Literacy* (American Association for the Advancement of Science) and John C. Bean's *Engaging Ideas*, "STEM education and WAC programs encourage interaction with society, evidence and reasoning in inquiry, application of knowledge, and engagement of students" (33). Two of our chapters in this collection focus specifically on science partnerships; one, a collaborative chapter, describes the partnership and its specific goals in relation to writing in science (Myelle-Watson et al.), while the other explains how a science teacher partners with others to improve writing, teaching and learning (Lowry).

Though less directly connected, but certainly influential in high school-college partnerships is academic achievement and college readiness testing. The ACT, SAT, and state-specific tests for high school graduation drive school curriculum decisions and influence college acceptance. The importance of the tests for students, teachers, schools, and districts, as well as colleges' use of tests in

11

admissions decisions, potentially casts a shadow over partnerships. And historically, the material tested does not align with the skills necessary for success in college (Hiss and Franks 2014). That may be changing, though. At the time of this writing, College Board has announced major changes in the SAT that will test students' knowledge based on what they have learned in secondary school, rather than what they should be able to do in college (Lewin 2014). Such changes also will continue over the years and should be impetus for even more secondary-postsecondary collaborations across the curriculum.

KINDS OF PARTNERSHIPS

In our research of existing partnerships, we discovered that many connect to statewide and community projects, dual credit courses, discipline-specific partnerships, volunteer professional organizations, writing centers, National Writing Project (NWP), pre-service through secondary education projects, and others including Advanced Placement (AP) and International Baccalaureate (IB) programs.

Community involvement is essential to the success of both secondary and postsecondary schools within a particular region. Just as the Tar River Writing Project (TRWP) collaboration with J. H. Rose High School in eastern North Carolina involved members of the community to act as mentors and role models in their Project Graduation, other public and private institutions do so in other ways. Henry Jenkins describes how "Participatory culture shifts the focus on literacy from one of individual expression to community involvement. The new literacies almost all involve social skills developed through collaboration and networking" (4). And, community may go beyond a physical region to a virtual one. In their digital literacy partnership, Bear, Estrem, Fredrickson, and Shepherd explain, "All of us are members of a larger 'participatory' culture that digital work makes possible" (132). In Trixie Smith's chapter of this collection, she describes short-term collaborations often work with community organizations.

As described in the Conference on College Composition and Communication (CCCC) 2012 position statement on dual credit/concurrent enrollment (DC/CE) courses, "state, national, and corporate leaders ... have identified DC/CE as one way ... to ensure 'college and career readiness' and a seamless bridge between secondary and postsecondary curricula assessment" (par. 1). College writing program administrators have focused on ensuring that high school teachers have credentials to teach college composition, and that course content in high schools is as rigorous as course content on college campuses (Hansen and Farris; Sullivan and Tinberg). National Alliance of Concurrent Enrollment Partnerships (NACEP), which began in 1999, is the accrediting organization for dual credit programs. Many states encourage accreditation from NACEP, and the standards may be found at http://www.nacep.org/accreditation/standards/ (Uhlenkamp 2014). In this collection, McMullen-Light includes a dual-credit teacher at the secondary school in her partnership in Chapter 6.

As previously mentioned, many of the partnerships described in this collection focus on writing in high school English and first-year composition classes; two focus on science connections. The collaborative work between the middle/high school teachers in Illinois with educators at Northern Illinois University (Chapter 5) demonstrates a clear desire to improve student learning that includes formative assessment with writing, rather than statewide assessment that occurs too late to make a difference in the learning of students in classes. By working as a team, educators can change that situation through a grassroots movement. Michael Lowry's personal experiences (Chapter 3) creating secondary-postsecondary partnerships through a variety of volunteer professional organizations remind readers that we don't have to wait for someone else to start such collaborations, and we don't have to wait for formal, institutional structures to be built; as professionals, all educators can discover ways to work together for the benefit of their own growth as teachers and the learning of their students. These examples can clearly be adapted to other disciplines as well.

In our research on partnerships, we discovered a wide variety of secondary-postsecondary writing center partnerships. In her research on the collaborative leadership qualities involved in six writing center partnerships in the United States, Julie Story notes the importance of exploration, power, and dynamics that enabled these partnerships to demonstrate the craft of human interdependence. She also mentions the resistance to change on the part of those outside the collaboration. Writing centers continue to be an ideal place to start WAC-based collaborations (Childers and Lowry, "Introduction"). The interaction among writing center directors and future directors through International Writing Centers Association (IWCA) annual summer institutes, as well as their state, regional and international conferences, allow partnerships to form in a variety of venues. In this collection Marie Hansen, Debra Hartley, Kirsten Jamsen, Katie Levin, and Kristen Nichols-Besel (Chapter 8) describe how one such partnership began and continues to grow and impact more writing centers on the secondary level. Many of the authors in this book, for instance, have met at several of these gatherings over the years and collaborated on other works as well. In fact, Luise Beaumont (Chapter 7), Kirsten Jamsen (Chapter 8) and Pam led a workshop on WAC Partnerships at the European Writing Centers Association conference at Viadrina University in Germany in July 2014.

As frequently as writing center partnerships were mentioned, many also connected to the National Writing Project. In fact, in many cases the two become clearly connected because of their similar beliefs in the value of WAC at all academic levels, the importance of student-centered practices, and their strong belief in teachers teaching teachers. The Tar River Writing Project partnership with J. H. Rose High School (JHR) is a perfect example. The school is described as having "struggled with racial parity and a higher than average dropout rate. In addition, JHR has struggled to graduate lower-achieving students, and increasing its graduation rate is a top priority for the school over the next few years" (West-Puckett and Banks 355-56). The principal and a few of the school's teacher-leaders called on Tar River Writing Project to help create a graduation project in which teachers could "conceptualize a curriculum that promotes (1) authentic inquiry, (2) experiential learning, and (3) making a doing—in short, a curriculum that provides rich literacy instruction with embedded opportunities to read, write, speak and listen in both virtual and face-to-face environments" (West-Puckett and Banks 358). Several authors in this collection have participated in and led National Writing Project sites near their institutions where participants in the institutes, as well as their leaders, represent all academic levels. Just "hanging out" for faculty development with professional colleagues from primary, secondary and postsecondary institutions breeds more partnerships.

In his article "The Persistence of Privacy: Autonomy and Initiative in Teachers' Professional Relations," J. W. Little emphasizes that true collaboration demands interdependence. Pre-service/secondary partnerships offer opportunities for just such interdependence. There is a natural progression from training for the educational profession to observing, then practice teaching, and eventually full-time teaching. At each of these stages, professional development and mentoring have essential roles while students are taking postsecondary courses as undergraduates and graduates, as well as within the very secondary institutions where they are teaching. Also, ongoing professional development means that teachers of secondary education courses, as well as the secondary teachers across the curriculum, must be aware of the latest challenges to teaching, the knowledge and social development of new generations of students from K-12, and beyond. Many of us have experienced an undergraduate or graduate school instructor referring to "when I was in school" in a similar way to what parents, politicians and other members of society say. That is not an acceptable response because advancements in all disciplines and societal changes require us as professional educators to be familiar with current pedagogical, educational, and global issues if we are to be effective in the classroom. Also, how are we to know the visions of future educational possibilities? How better to know what is happening and what constraints classroom teachers face than partnering with them?

The chapters in this volume share and celebrate various WAC partnership manifestations that vary from frameworks to build connectivity between institutions while addressing Common Core State Standards (Chapter 2), to academic and non-academic collaborations around science education (Chapter 3), to two chapters on non-North American WAC partnerships (Chapters 4 and 7), and an argument for short-term collaborations (Chapter 9). As you examine the book, you will see it is broken into three broad sections: Unique Programs, Process-Based Programs, and Writing Center-Based Programs. Although most chapters are unique processes that may involve writing centers, we tried to organize them into these individual sections for emphasis; however, they all represent models that are replicable once accommodations are made for local contexts.

In the first chapter of the Unique Programs section, Michelle Cox and Phyllis Gimbel (Chapter 2) detail their using WACommunities as a framework to bring secondary and post-secondary educators across disciplinary boundaries together to discuss what the Common Core State Standards will mean for writing instruction in different disciplines and their implications for teaching writing across the curriculum and across the secondary-post-secondary divide. Chapter 3, by Michael Lowry, discusses several partnerships that he initiated, including the creation of a NASA-sponsored online course, interdisciplinary activity among science, art and English teachers through Project Zero at Harvard, and interactions within volunteer professional organizations such as National Science Teachers Association. All of these projects involve collaboration with post-secondary communities. The emphasis of the chapter is to place these specific examples in the larger context of creating connections between secondary and postsecondary institutions that have an impact on WAC for teachers to improve student learning. The final chapter of the section (Chapter 4) by Federico Navarro and Andrea Revel Chion describes the writing program at a high school, which is an innovative literacy project that has critically adapted the WAC perspective in the initial and advanced course of a high school in Buenos Aires, Argentina. In addition, it discusses how the project addresses some of WAC's major challenges when implemented in a middle/high school.

The Process-Based Programs section begins with a chapter by Danielle Myelle-Watson, Deb Spears, David Wellen, Michael McClellan, and Brad Peters about a grant-funded partnership that studied the use of writing-to-learn activities to develop critical thinking strategies in ninth-grade science classrooms. The chapter describes the challenge of accommodating the unexpected to maintain and value the partnership. It tells of the struggles secondary teachers have and the thoughtful ways in which they modified their teaching to accommodate competing needs and interests. Mary McMullen-Light, in Chapter 6, provides readers with the genesis and development of a partnership that spans the secondary-postsecondary divide. McMullen-Light explains the seemingly unlikely partnership and how some shared fundamental goals the educators have for their students results in a successful and meaningful collaboration that establishes a sustainable high school writing center and valuable WAC professional development opportunities for both the community college and the high school. The last chapter of the Process-Based Programs section is by Luise Beaumont, Mandy Pydde, and Simone Tschirpke. They examine the expectations and communication issues surrounding a collaboration between a German university and a German high school. The project partnered university staff and peer tutors with high school tutors to develop a WAC-based peer tutoring center in the high school. Though the project did not go as planned, the authors learned much about differing expectations and how to negotiate them.

The final section, Writing Center-Based Programs, begins with an inspiring collaboration between Burnsville High School and the University of Minnesota. The authors, Marie Hansen, Debra Hartley, Kirsten Jamsen, Katie Levin, and Kristen Nichols-Besel, tell a compelling story of a cold-call request for a visit to bring the high school tutors to the University of Minnesota. From there the collaboration grew into relationship building, professional development, and deep friendships, and the authors share the experience and the lessons learned. In Chapter 9, long-term partnerships are the ultimate goal. Trixie Smith demonstrates that sometimes partners just need a jumpstart, a little help in conceiving of and planning for the possibilities, to get started with new programming. Short-term partnerships also have the advantage of low costs, low commitments, and fewer logistical problems. Despite these low-stakes investments, the payoff can be rich and rewarding for area teachers, students, and community members, as well as the WAC-based writing center, its staff, and the university.

In the concluding chapter of the book, we zoom out to comment on the broader trends that emerge from the chapters of this book, as well as survey data about additional partnerships not included in this volume. We also offer some possible directions partnerships might head in the future and how they can be nurtured to offer meaningful experiences for students, teachers, and scholars. We believe the book offers educators valuable models of high school-college partnerships and analyses of the experiences of those involved. There are many barriers to bridging the divide between K-12 and college, but the need to develop partnerships is as great as it has ever been. Finally, we believe the myriad of successes showcased in these pages offer readers hope that WAC partnerships are possible, necessary and inspiring.

WORKS CITED

American Association for the Advancement of Science. *Atlas of Science Literacy*. 2 vols. Washington: AAAS Project 2061, 2011. Print.

Bean, John C. *Engaging Ideas*. 2nd ed. San Francisco: Jossey-Bass, 2011. Print.

Bear, Rachel, Heidi Estrem, James E. Fredricksen, and Dawn Shepherd. "Participation and Collaboration in Digital Spaces: Connecting High School and College Writing Experiences." *The Next Digital Scholar: A Fresh Approach to the Common Core State Standards in Research and Writing*. Ed. James P. Purdy and Randall McClure. MedfordAmerican Society for Information Science and Technology, 2014. 131-74. Print.

Bernstein, Kenneth. "Warnings from the Trenches." *Academe* 99.1 (2013): 32-36. Web.

Blumner, Jacob, and Pamela Childers. "Building Better Bridges: What Makes High School-College WAC Collaborations Work?" *The WAC Journal* 22 (2011): 91-101. Web. 1 Nov. 2014.

Childers, Pamela B., and Michael J. Lowry. "Introduction to Writing Across the Curriculum in Secondary Schools." *Across the Disciplines* 9.3 (2012): n. page. Web. 25 July 2013.

---. "STEMing the Tide: Writing to Learn in Science." *Cases on Inquiry through Instructional Technology in Math and Science*. Ed. Lesia C. Lennex and Kimberely Fletcher Nettleton. Hershey, PA: IGI Global, 2012. Web. 30 Sept. 2014.

Clift, Renée, Mary Lou Veal, Marlene Johnson, and Patricia Holland. "Restructuring Teacher Education through Collaborative Action Research." *Journal of Teacher Education* 41.2 (1990): 52-62. Web.

Conference on College Composition and Communication. "Statement Dual Credit/Concurrent Enrollment Composition: Policy and Best Practices." Nov. 2012. Web. 30 Sept. 2014.

Cox, Michelle, and Phyllis Gimbel. "Conversations Among Teachers on Student Writing: WAC/Secondary Education Partnerships at BSU." *Across the Disciplines: A Journal of Language, Learning, and Academic Writing*. The WAC Clearinghouse. 8 Dec. 2012. Web. 30 Sept. 2014.

Digby, Annette D., Barbara C. Gartin, and Nikki L. Murdick. "Developing Effective University and Public School Partnerships." *The Clearing House: A Journal of Educational Strategies, Issues and Ideas* 67.1 (1993): 37-39. Web. 30 Sept. 2014.

Hansen, Kristine, & Christine Farris, eds. College Credit for Writing in High School: The "Taking Care of" Business. Urbana, IL: NCTE, 2010. Print.

Hiss, William C., and Valerie W. Franks. *Defining Promise: Optional Standardized Testing Policies in American College and University Admissions*. National Association for College Admissions Counseling. 2 Feb. 2014. Web. 30 Sept. 2014.

Jenkins, Henry. *Confronting the Challenges of Participatory Culture: Media Education for the 21st Century*. Massachusetts Institute of Technology. Cambridge:

MIT P, 2009. Web. 30 Sept. 2014.

Knowles, Malcolm. *Andragogy in Action: Applying Modern Principles of Adult Learning*. San Francisco: Jossey-Bass, 1984. Print.

Lewin, Tamar. "A New SAT Aims to Align with Schoolwork." *New York Times* 5 Mar. 2014. Web. 30 Sept. 2014.

Little, J. W. "The Persistence of Privacy: Autonomy and Initiative in Teachers' Professional Relations." *Teachers College Record* 91 (1990): 509-36. Print.

Lunsford, Andrea A., and Karen J. Lunsford. "'Mistakes are a Fact of Life': A National Comparative Study." *CCC* 59.4 (2008): 781–806. Web.

McDaniel, Kathryn Noble. "Read Long and Prosper: Five Do's and Don'ts for Preparing Students for College." *The Clearing House* 87.2 (2014): 83-87. Print.

Reynolds, Candyce, Dannelle D. Stevens, and Ellen West. "'I'm in a Professional School! Why Are You Making Me Do This?' A Cross-Disciplinary Study of the Use of Creative Classroom Projects on Student Learning." *College Teaching* 61 (2013): 51-59. Web.

Story, Julie A. "Leaders' Experiences with High School-College Writing Center Collaborations: A Qualitative Multiple-Case Study." Diss. U of Phoenix. 2014. Print.

Sullivan, Patrick, & Howard Tinberg, eds. *What is "College-Level" Writing?* Urbana: National Council of Teachers of English, 2011. Print.

Teaching Institute for Excellence in STEM (TIES). (2011). "*What is STEM Education?*" 2014. Web. 30 Sept. 2014.

Uhlenkamp, James. "RE: Thanks." Message to Pamela Childers. 21 June 2014. Email.

West-Puckett, Stephanie, and William P. Banks. "UnCommon Connections: How Building a Grass-Roots Curriculum Helped Reframe Common Core State Standards for Teachers and Students in a High Need Public High School." *The Next Digital Scholar: A Fresh Approach to the Common Core State Standards in Research and Writing*. Ed. James P. Purdy and Randall McClure. Medford: American Society for Information Science and Technology, 2014. 353-83. Print.

CHAPTER 2

TALKING ABOUT WRITING ACROSS THE SECONDARY AND COLLEGE COMMUNITY

Michelle Cox and Phyllis Gimbel

Many have commented that higher education is becoming increasingly fragmented, leading to the overspecialization of scholars, disciplinary discourses that are opaque to those outside the field, and lack of cross-pollination among disciplines (Kerr). WAC has long been seen as a movement that creates connections among disciplines. In fact, these connections are often created through the workshop, the quintessential WAC experience, as it "bring[s] faculty together around the same table" —bringing together people who may work at the same institution but, in practice, work worlds apart (Cox 317). More recently, this movement to bring people around the same table has come to include colleagues from secondary education (Childers and Lowry).

While this practice of WAC has long been recognized, it has not been adequately theorized. Writing Across Communities (WACommunities), introduced by Michelle Hall Kells and Juan C. Guerra, was developed to rethink student writing. This approach to WAC asks us to think of student writing holistically, as including students' literacy and language experiences outside of the classroom—online writing, civic writing, disciplinary writing, writing in languages other than English—as well as the writing students did before they entered our classrooms and what they'll write after leaving them. In this chapter, we argue that WACommunities is also a productive theory for reconceptualizing relationships among educators, drawing on an event we organized at Bridgewater State University (BSU) as an example of this theory in practice.

WRITING ACROSS COMMUNITIES: FROM STUDENTS TO EDUCATORS

Writing Across Communities (or, WACommunities) is a conceptual framework developed by Kells for the WAC initiative at the University of New Mexico. Inspired in part by Steve Parks and Eli Goldblatt's "Writing beyond the Curriculum: Fostering New Collaborations in Literacy," the UNM WACommunities program intentionally reaches across multiple sites and types of writing. Kells tells us:

> WAC is not a single conversation. It is a ganglion of conversations that links to an ever-expanding range of practices and intellectual pursuits: computer-mediated writing instruction, service learning, writing-intensive courses, first-year writing seminars, technical and professional writing, interdisciplinary learning communities, writing centers, ESL and bilingual education, and many more. (91)

Here, the emphasis is on types of writing and programs that are included within the scope of a university curriculum. But Kells' view of WAC is more expansive than this: "I contend that traditional models of WAC too narrowly privilege academic discourse over other discourses and communities shaping the worlds in which our students live and work" (Kells 93). We would add that WAC has too narrowly privileged *college-level* academic discourse, a view supported by Juan Guerra, who describes traditional WAC programs as having a "too-limited and limiting focus on language, literacy, and learning *within the university itself*" (emphasis added, 298).

We can see that Kells' vision for WAC is focused on students—the students' experiences of literacy across writing programs and within disciplines, but also beyond the curriculum, across the myriad writing, reading, and language experiences in daily lives. With this article, we use this same inclusive approach when considering faculty. Too often, educators are separated by level and by discipline. How often is it that secondary school teachers and college teachers—who may be teaching down the road from each other—meet and talk about teaching? How often is it that even educators in the same discipline from different levels—say a math high school teacher and a college professor teaching the same subject—meet? Our students traverse secondary and higher education, but the teachers who work with them often only meet teachers within their own institution, and, at conferences, specialists in their disciplines who teach at the same level. WACommunities, as conceived by Kells, reconceptualizes writing by decompartmentalizing it. This approach to WAC, thus, can be used to broaden our view of the communities we perceive as within the scope of a university WAC program, namely the teachers who mentor literacy beyond the university curriculum.

Doing so benefits all involved. For secondary schools, participation in university WAC programs provides models for WAC programming, a need emerging as schools struggle to meet the Common Core State Standards (CCSS), which compels content area teachers across the curriculum to include writing as a focus of instruction. Moreover, as CCSS emphasizes college readiness, inclusion of secondary school teachers in university WAC programs creates opportunities for these teachers to learn more about current college curricula. WAC programs also benefit from contact with secondary teachers. As we argued in "Conversations among Teachers on Student Writing: WAC/Secondary Education Partnerships at BSU," "In order to create effective programming, we need to know more about the kinds of experiences with writing students have had before arriving on campus" (Cox and Gimbel n. pag.).

This goal of learning about student writing experiences before they arrive at the university fits with the philosophy of WACommunities. Guerra argues, "the focus of traditional WAC programs and initiatives on writing across academic programs has left under-examined the experiences students bring with them from their earlier grades in school and the varied out-of-school communities that all of our students inhabit" (298). He states that WACommunities addresses this issue by "argu[ing] that teachers and contexts can play critical roles in a student's ability to use the prior knowledge and experiences that every student brings from previous communities of practice to any social or cultural setting" (Guerra 298). As writing becomes embedded in content areas across the curriculum, it will become even more important for secondary teachers and college faculty from the same field to become acquainted with how writing is used and taught in their respective classrooms, so that secondary teachers can help their students prepare for college-level writing-in-the-disciplines (WID), and so that college faculty can help students utilize what they learned about WID before entering college.

The panel event we describe later in this chapter was designed to begin this exchange among content-area teachers in secondary schools in southeastern Massachusetts and faculty at Bridgewater State University (BSU) teaching in the same discipline at the college level. During the event, we also distributed an IRB-approved questionnaire surveying the participants' responses to the event, as well as their responses to CCSS, which was used as a focal point for the event. Below, we provide background on our local context, describe the panel event in more detail, and analyze participant responses to the event and to CCSS, ending the chapter with a discussion of how WACommunities and CCSS can continue to frame secondary education-university WAC discussions and collaborations.

WAC AT BRIDGEWATER STATE UNIVERSITY

The event we describe below, which was held in April 2012, was one in a series of events and programs that brought together secondary education teachers and BSU faculty through the BSU WAC program (for more details, see Cox and Gimbel). The WAC program at BSU, a regional university in southeastern Massachusetts enrolling about 11,000 students, was launched in spring 2007 by Michelle Cox. BSU, unlike many universities, did not have a history of started, stopped, and restarted WAC programs—this was the first attempt to initiate a WAC program at BSU. Further, at BSU, WAC is not directly tied to the general education curriculum. It provides support for the writing-intensive courses mandated by the university's latest reform to general education, but is not limited to working with this program. Therefore, without these restraints in place, Michelle felt free to not limit the scope of the program to the undergraduate curriculum, the traditional scope of university WAC programs, but to instead develop the program's scope in response to needs she observed. The BSU WAC program would come to include support for graduate student writing, support for faculty writing (Cox and Brunjes), and a series of programming focused on connecting secondary and college educators. (This series was informed by Michelle's participation in Pamela Childers and Jacob Blumner's pre-conference workshop on WAC-secondary education collaborations at the 2010 IWAC Conference, a workshop also described in Hansen, Hartely, Jamsen, Levin, and Nichols-Besel in Chapter 8).

Secondary-education related programming was strengthened in 2010 when Phyllis Gimbel, a secondary education leadership professor and former secondary school language teacher and middle school principal, joined the WAC program as assistant coordinator. Phyllis spearheaded a series of secondary education-university events (Cox and Gimbel), including the panel event that is the focus of this article.

PANEL EVENT AT BSU: "THE TRANSITION FROM HIGH SCHOOL TO COLLEGE WRITING: COMMON CORE STATE STANDARDS"

The focus of this panel event emerged from discussions with area secondary school teachers and feedback to other secondary education-university WAC events. Again and again, we heard from teachers that they wanted to talk about the impact of CCSS on student work and teaching, and hear about student writing across academic levels and disciplines. A group that was critical in helping us plan this event was a group convened by BSU English education specialist John Kucich, who organized monthly meetings of high school and college English teachers. The high school teachers at this meeting emphasized the fact that neither secondary nor college teachers knew what kinds of writing was assigned at other levels, and that high school teachers in particular would be interested in seeing samples of student writing from college content areas. As English teachers, they were seen as having the responsibility of introducing writing instruction to the social studies, math, and science teachers, and yet they did not know what writing would look like in the disciplines. This group also helped us make decisions about the timing and format of the event. With their help, we planned for an after-school panel discussion that included opportunities for group discussions and ended with dinner and another opportunity for cross-level conversation.

CCSS is not only a focus of practicing teachers. As we began looking for collaborators in hosting the event, we learned that the BSU College of Education and Allied Studies (CEAS) was under pressure to provide programming focused on CCSS. When we met with the CEAS dean, she immediately offered to fully fund the event, advertise the event, and handle registration. This was welcome news, as the WAC program had been level-funded that year and the dinner requested by our secondary school colleagues had not been part of the initial budget. Further, we, as WAC administrators, didn't have access to administrative assistants for such tasks as advertising and registration.

With the funding and administrative issues under control, Phyllis could focus on pulling together a cross-level and cross-disciplinary panel. For the panel, Phyllis recruited representation from secondary schools—a middle school social studies teacher who was also enrolled as a graduate student at our university, a high school English department chair, and a public school director of instruction and assessment and former graduate of our institution. Phyllis also included administrators and faculty from BSU: the CEAS dean, our WAC Coordinator (Michelle), an assistant professor of mathematics, and an assistant professor of math education. The dean was asked to give a brief overview of CCSS, which was particularly important for those in the audience from higher education, and Michelle was asked to wrap up the panel discussion. The other four panelists were asked to, in seven minutes, respond to the following prompts:

1. What is the role of writing in your field (social studies/history, science, math, English/language arts)?
2. Show/provide us with an example of a writing activity or student writing from your classroom.
3. How do you see the CCSS standards impacting what you are doing now with writing in your classrooms?

On the day of the event, eighty local secondary school educators and administrators, college faculty and administrators, and pre-service teachers gathered for this cross-institutional and cross-level discussion of student writing, WAC, and CCSS. The presenters talked candidly about their concerns about CCSS and shared their teaching practices related to writing. From our perspective, it was quite wonderful to see student writing, often handwritten, projected on the big screen, as well as to hear how faculty from different disciplines saw writing as integral to teaching and learning. Indeed, many of the samples of student writing shared by presenters were from writing-to-learn activities (an emphasis also shared by Navarro and Chion, Chapter 4). Based on responses on the IRB-approved questionnaire we distributed after the event,[1] many of the participants also saw these aspects as the highlights of the event. Here is a sampling of responses to the question, "What from today's event impacted you the most?":

- Examples of student work. [elementary school teacher and BSU graduate student[2]]
- The writing occurring here at BSU across the curriculum. [secondary school teacher, special education]
- The sample math writing examples were interesting. [high school teacher, English]
- Seeing student samples of writing. [secondary school teacher, visual arts]
- The examples of science and math writing. [secondary school administrator, curriculum director]
- All the great ways writing is being used in math learning about the CCSS. [college teacher, English]
- Examples of really rich writing in different disciplines – there are lots of great opportunities for engaging, meaningful writing. [college teacher, English]

Here, it is clear that just seeing actual student writing was important to both secondary and college faculty, while it was seeing samples from disciplines other than their own, such as math and science, that most impacted them. In response to the same question, others spoke more holistically about the impact of the event:

- Hearing from the teachers and speakers who have great creative ideas that are working in the classroom. [middle school teacher, history]
- The willingness of other disciplines (other than English) to embrace the ideas of WAC. [high school teacher, English]
- Confidence that we can handle this. [high school teacher, history]
- The sense of optimism that radiates from this kind of dialogue [high school teacher, English]
- The acknowledgement that writing is a complex thought process that needs opportunity for practice and specific feedback in a timely manner. [high school teacher, English]

- Seeing what other schools are currently doing made me aware that our school is way behind when it comes to preparing for CCSS [and] when it comes to WAC. [high school department head, science]
- Ideas to incorporate in my teaching practice. [college teacher, early childhood education]
- I was pleased that the conversation is beginning in academic departments other than just English (although I appreciate the idea that writing is everyone's responsibility now). I like that math and other departments will also be conducting seminars/conversations. [college teacher, English]
- It was very valuable to hear from teachers and administrators from a wide variety of districts sharing their concerns and ideas surrounding the Common Core. It was a good "zeitgeist-capturing moment" for me, since I'm not often involved in wider conversations around writing, teaching writing, and the K-12 curriculum. [college teacher, mathematics]

Though the event was designed to facilitate conversation between secondary and college faculty teaching in the same discipline, most respondents focused instead on the value of cross-disciplinary conversation. Based on these comments, we can see that both secondary school and college faculty were inspired by the ways in which writing is taught in fields other than their own. In particular, English teachers at both the high school and college level appreciated seeing faculty from fields other than English taking responsibility for teaching writing. Further, both high school and college faculty commented that just being part of the conversation was valuable, either to get a sense of where their own institution stood in relation to WAC programming (as expressed by the high school science department head), or because such opportunities are rare (as expressed by the college math professor).

We also asked participants to comment on what they would want as a focus for future workshops. Respondents' comments centered on specific teaching practices (i.e., designing writing assignments, assessing writing), seeing writing from more disciplines (such as music and art), spending more time on specific disciplines (such as English or history), and using a workshop structure in place of a panel, in order to facilitate more small group discussions and hands-on activities. This year's panel discussion was followed by a question and answer session, small-group discussions, and dinner, which provided more opportunities for conversation, which was a change from the previous year's program in response to requests for more interaction. It is clear that the participants desired even more time for interaction. Further, not all participants remained for activities that followed the panel discussion. Many public school teachers, tired from a day that often begins before 7 a.m., wanted to go home to their families for dinner, and they did not stay for dinner or for small group discussion and materials exchange.

RESPONSES TO CCSS

We also used this event as an opportunity to learn more about how educators in secondary and higher education thought about CCSS, as we felt that it was important that the panelists' perspectives on CCSS were not the only ones expressed during this event. Kells criticizes "traditional WAC approaches" for "replicat[ing] and reaffirm[ing] dominant discourses by socializing new writers into established systems" (93). In keeping with WACommunities, in our work with educators, we didn't want the WAC program to be positioned as fully supporting CCSS, a dominant discourse present in secondary education, but as interrogating it and as providing space for public dialogue. Further, traditionally, the secondary school-university relationship is one of uneven power, with secondary education teachers tasked with preparing students to meet the expectations of college teachers, a dynamic reified by the CCSS's emphasis on college readiness. In addition to the other opportunities provided by this event, the questionnaire created a space where each participant could voice his/her point of view.

Before sharing the responses, it is important to provide some context on the history of standardized testing in Massachusetts, where our institution is located. In this state, the teaching of writing in public schools, especially public schools in under-resourced districts, has been largely shaped by standardized testing, particularly the Massachusetts Comprehensive Assessment System (MCAS). Students take MCAS tests in grades one, three, five, seven, and nine, with the sophomore test determining high school graduation, and test scores at each level impacting school funding and ranking of teachers. Writing in MCAS tests is restricted to two genres: an "open response," which is a response to a question based on a short reading, and a "long composition," which is a five-paragraph thesis-driven essay (for more details, see Cox and Gimbel). Some of the more positive perspectives on CCSS expressed by some of the secondary school participants may surprise readers familiar with the criticisms of CCSS for not stressing rhetoric's relation to writing, but the varied genres and purposes of writing as represented in CCSS are richer than in MCAS, the point of comparison for many who participated in this event.

Below, we list each question and then share and discuss sample responses.

How has/will the new Common Core State Standards impact you? How will it affect the ways you write/teach writing/administer a program?

Some respondents from K-12 talked about CCSS as *forcing* change:

- Have to incorporate more writing in my subject area (music). [elementary school teacher in music and BSU graduate student]
- Force me to move history closer to English through writing, research, and discipline. [secondary school teacher, history]
- This will force my school to emphasize argumentation far more. [high school teacher, English]

Others in K-12 discussed how CCSS will have widespread impact:

- They will change my curriculum. It will involve training, more professional development, and different pedagogy. [secondary school teacher, subject not provided]
- The CCSS impact the ways I will administer a program by giving writing assignments for every art assignment. [secondary school teacher, art]
- These standards will have a major impact. They will permeate the assessments, interaction, and activities in the classroom. The standards will give impetus for a history teacher to look critically at student writing. Collaboration will be of the utmost importance among faculty. [BSU graduate student, accelerated postbaccalaureate program]
- Greater focus on helping teachers in other disciplines incorporate reading and writing, by providing professional development in reading and writing pedagogy. [secondary school administrator, curriculum director]

Here, we hear the respondents discussing how writing will now be emphasized in disciplines outside of English, specifically in history and art. We hear faculty development and collaboration among teachers from different disciplines emphasized. Change is emphasized, but the change isn't necessarily cast in a negative or positive light. In contrast, respondents from higher education seemed to see CCSS as facilitating their understanding of the writing knowledge and experience students will enter college with:

- I teach critical writing at the college level and believe that a better understanding of the students' previous high school training will help me model the class more effectively. [college teacher, theater]
- It will impact me in terms of what students arrive in first-year writing

expecting and how well prepared they are for the variety of assignments they'll encounter. [college teacher, English]
- It has not yet, but it will in Fall 2012 when I teach a FYS [first-year seminar] course. I am very pleased to see this broad based approach to THINKING and writing. [college teacher, criminal justice]

As, at the time of this writing, 45 states, the District of Columbia, and four U.S. territories have adopted CCSS (Common Core), they indeed hold the promise of allowing college educators to have a better sense of the writing education of their first-year students, as students from states from different sections of the country will purportedly emphasize the same writing standards. This standardization may be especially helpful for colleges that enroll students and hire faculty from across the country.

How do you think that the new Common Core State Standards will impact students' transition from high school to college writing?

Overall, responses to this question were positive. Some responses indicated that students should be better prepared to meet the challenges of college writing:

- I think college students' writing will become more thoughtful. [BSU graduate student, English]
- It should create a more seamless transition as the writing should be more precise and at a higher level. [secondary school teacher, subject not provided]
- I think it will better prepare them for the rigor of college courses. [high school department head, science]
- CCSS will change the nature of students' understanding of what can be accomplished in writing. I expect that in 8-10 years that entering [college] freshmen will have a better sense of the relationships of audience, purpose, and genre to writing. [college teacher, English]

Others focused on how students will be better prepared to write across the college curriculum:

- When faced with science and history reading/writing, students will be more prepared. [high school teacher, science]
- Will require students to develop and practice writing skills in many different disciplines. [high school department head, science]

Some responses from secondary school teachers focused on how the increased communication between high school and college teachers will ease the transition for student writers:

- I am hopeful that we as secondary teachers will be able to more adequately prepare students as college professors expect them to be prepared. [high school teacher, English]
- I hope it will make the transition smoother for them as college educators gain a better understanding of what level of training to expect from incoming students from MA. [secondary school teacher, special education]

Three respondents alluded to MCAS in their responses:

- My fear is that non-English teachers will rely on traditional, formulaic writing (i.e., 5 paragraph essays, MCAS style open response). [high school department head, history]
- [The transition will be] difficult at first as so much has fallen back because of teaching to test ... CCSS will bring it back and in the end transition will be much more smooth. [secondary school teacher, English]
- It would seem to make the transition more natural by exposing students to a wider variety of writing styles and purposes than MCAS has so far. This should benefit them in their first-year writing and first-year seminar courses especially, permitting them to focus more on the acquisition of college-success (study and research) skills and rhetoric rather than on composition. [college teacher, mathematics]

MCAS writing, with its focus on form over rhetoric and content, encouraged a teaching-to-the-test approach. As one high school teacher said when describing writing instruction in an urban school under MCAS, "I find in my class that I'm teaching to the test right now. I'm drilling on five paragraph essays, lots of thesis statements, transitional sentences—talking about things I've always talked about, but now I'm drilling constantly" (Luna and Turner 83). Writing, as described in CCSS, is richer and more varied, but at the time of this event, assessments of the CCSS have not yet been implemented,[3] and it is the test of standards, even more than the standards themselves, that often shape pedagogy, a concern that was raised in response to the next question.

What concerns do you have about the Common Core State Standards?

As one respondent answered succinctly, CCSS raised concerns about, "implementation, assessment, time, budget." Some of the responses spoke to the fatigue that comes with being frequently required to adopt new curriculum imposed by the state or district. As one respondent wrote:

- I'm concerned that this is just yet another trendy initiative being driven by corporate America to force school systems and governments to spend untold millions of dollars on new texts, tests, programs, etc., only for us to find out in 10 years that students derived no benefits from it. [high school department head, English]

This response indicates a key difference in teaching at the secondary and college level. In general, college faculty have far more leverage on curriculum than do their colleagues in secondary education (a generalization that does not hold in secondary schools outside of the US; see, for instance, the faculty-led writing program described by Navarro and Chion, Chapter 4, in which teachers can opt to participate). In higher education, it is widely recognized that WAC programs developed as grassroots efforts are more successful and sustainable than those imposed by administration. The WAC initiatives in secondary education compelled by CCSS can hardly be seen as grassroots initiatives, as CCSS are adopted at the state level.

Other responses spoke to concerns that those administering WAC programs in college will readily recognize. Some of the responses focused on the issue of faculty development:

- Millions of teachers will require professional development. [respondent did not provide information on position]
- Training for the non-English teachers [will be needed]. [BSU graduate student, accelerated post-baccalaureate program]
- It may be difficult for other content areas to become accustomed to integrating literacy instruction. [high school teacher, English]

Others spoke to balancing time for content and writing:

- I am concerned that "lines" between subjects (English to math) may become more "blurred" or not defined. This may become a very large challenge when math subject content has to be eliminated to reach standards. [secondary school teacher, visual arts]

For English language arts (ELA) educators, the new challenge is in balancing literary and non-literary texts, as this respondent noted:

- Striking a balance between literature exploration and authentic assessments of non-fiction. [high school teacher, English]

The new standards for ELA emphasize expository (rather than literary) reading and writing, with 70% of a student's reading and writing tasks to be focused on nonfiction texts by the senior year of high school (National Assessment Governing Board). This 70% refers to the whole curriculum, not just the English classroom, but ELA teachers will share part of this responsibility.

The concerns these educators express are legitimate, and indicate roles that college WAC programs can have in supporting WAC initiates in secondary schools. Danielle Lillge, writing about the opportunities for WAC created by CCSS, states, "CCSS offer WAC advocates new possibilities for positively contributing possible solutions and professional knowledge to the challenges secondary teachers and schools face" (n. pag.). As we argued in a previous publication (Cox and Gimbel), college-level WAC programs have a wealth of experience in initiating cross-disciplinary conversations about writing, offering faculty development on writing, and guiding faculty across the disciplines in integrating content with writing. Instructors of writing-intensive courses, such as the math faculty featured in our panel discussion, can share approaches to integrating writing-to-learn and writing-to-communicate pedagogies with content-area peers in secondary schools. Instructors of first-year writing and first-year seminars often have a wealth of experience in teaching with non-fiction texts and can share this knowledge with secondary school ELA teachers. This WAC knowledge, gained over years of WAC work in higher education, is now welcomed by secondary education as they grapple with CCSS, which Lillge describes as creating a critical moment for WAC in secondary education:

> Never before has secondary WAC been mandated with such wholesale scope and fervor across the United States. Whereas previous crises conversations had resulted in recommendations that allowed individual states and school districts to decide whether or not they chose to adopt these suggestions (e.g., Bazerman et al., 2005; Russell, 2009; Sheils, 1975), those states that have adopted the CCSS leave no option for school districts' voluntary adoption. Like no other historic moment, the CCSS has required a new level of buy-in and new possibility for secondary WAC. (n. pag.)

What do you see as the benefits of the Common Core State Standards?

Many of the comments on the benefits of CCSS touched on the same topics that had been raised as concerns. For example, respondents who teach at the college-level saw the new emphasis on non-literary texts and argument as positive:

- More focus on informational/content oriented texts. [college teacher, subject not provided]
- Focus on non-literary texts and argumentative writing. [college teacher, English]

Other respondents from both secondary schools and BSU saw the interdisciplinary approach advocated by CCSS not as threatening the content of disciplines, but enhancing education:

- The CCSS also invites all teachers to become teachers of reading and writing, recognizing that skills are used differently in a variety of content areas and we owe it to our students to prepare them to continue to acquire knowledge and skill independently, regardless of their future intentions for work or study. [high school teacher, English]
- It can benefit all subjects and create collaboration among teachers. [BSU graduate student, English]
- Students win a common language among disciplines and therefore transferable. [high school department head, science]
- A serious attempt to integrate learning. I think because academia is so narrowly focused with disciplines very much separated from each other that students are short-changed. The real world is interdisciplinary; academia is not. [college teacher, criminal justice]
- They foster a WAC approach—reading and writing outside of ELA is a real emphasis. They foster conversation among disciplines and levels (especially secondary—college). [college teacher, English]

Some respondents focused on the consistency created by the standards and the formative approach of the standards:

- [The standards] are detailed and apply across the curriculum. [secondary school teacher, special education]
- The uniform standard of measurement it will provide to let us compare realistically the scores of students in different states. [high school department head, English]
- Consistency at all the schools. [college teacher, English]
- The focus on college readiness (rather than high-school completion) makes this more a "formative" set of standards rather than a "summative" set of standards, which will only benefit students looking forward. It also makes intentional the idea that colleges and high schools should be in conversation with one another to smooth students' transition. [college teacher, mathematics]

Other responses focused on the benefits gleaned from an increased focus on writing:

- Higher level thinking. [elementary school teacher, music, and BSU graduate student]

- More critical thinking and improved literacy. [secondary school teacher, subject not provided]
- A benefit to promote critical thinking, which is needed not only in educational environment but in the workforce of the nation. [secondary school teacher, visual arts]
- It focuses on the rhetorical force in writing and on writing as an aid to developing thought. [college teacher, English]

It could be that this last set of responses were prompted by the focus of the event—writing—but the benefits from increased practice with writing as a mode of learning and writing as a mode of communication, in varied genres, and for varied audiences and purposes, have long been recognized by WAC.

CONCLUSION

From our perspective, as the organizers of this event and other secondary education-WAC programming, these responses on CCSS are useful, in that they help us determine directions for future exploration. For instance, what are the connections among writing, critical thinking, and interdisciplinarity? What kinds of activities and assignments promote writing as an "aid to developing thought" at the secondary level and college level? What can college WAC programs do to assist area school districts as they develop WAC initiatives? What can college WAC programs learn from the ways in which secondary schools develop WAC pedagogies and programs? And what kinds of cross-level events on writing can facilitate conversations on these topics?

Events such as this one are certainly a step in facilitating cross-disciplinary and cross-level discussions of WAC, but as we know from WAC lore (and also attested to by McMullen-Light, Chapter 6), a single workshop, without follow-up, does not have much impact. We are happy to report that, since holding this event, even though Michelle has taken a position at another university and Phyllis' term as assistant WAC coordinator has ended, WAC secondary school-university collaborations have continued at BSU. Throughout the 2012-2013 academic year, the group of ELA teachers and college faculty convened by John Kucich (mentioned above) continued to meet to talk about student writing and exchange teaching materials. John Kucich graciously served as interim WAC director following Michelle's leave, and led the third annual Transition from High School to College Writing panel event, this time featuring a middle school ELA teacher, a high school ELA program director, a BSU librarian, and the director of BSU's First and Second Year Seminar Program (a program that includes writing-intensive themed courses taught by faculty across the curriculum).

In light of WACommunities, it would be important that these ongoing conversations about student writing include investigation into students. WACommunities is an approach to WAC that focuses not only on kinds of writing and locations of writing, but also on the writers themselves: their linguistic, class, racial, ethnic, and socio-economic backgrounds. Regional colleges such as BSU, with enrollments drawn largely from local high schools, could learn a great deal about their students by opening conversations on issues of student diversity with colleagues from local school districts. These conversations could be especially useful in investigating linguistic diversity, as most institutions of higher education collect information about international students but not resident students who use English as a second language (L2). Regional colleges, particularly those in areas rich in immigrant communities, such as BSU, tend to enroll more resident L2 students than international students. Working with secondary education colleagues to co-investigate local L2 student populations would only benefit all involved, especially as linguistic background is important to the teaching and learning of writing.

The WACommunities approach and CCSS both open opportunities for secondary school-higher education collaborations and conversations. WACommunities, with its focus on writing across the many communities that students traverse within college, across school levels, across languages, and across their daily lives, compels educators to have a more expansive view of writing, as well as to reach out to educators teaching the same students, whether in different disciplines, different grade levels, or different institutions. CCSS, with its emphasis on writing in different content areas and, in ELA, on non-literary texts, prompts cross-disciplinary and cross-level conversations on writing, and, as argued by Lillge, creates a moment when interest in WAC is at a peak in secondary education. The panel event described in this article is but one response to the call by secondary schools for cross-level dialogue with college WAC programs on student writing. College-level WAC programs can play an important role in assisting secondary schools in negotiating CCSS, as well as interrogating these state-issued mandates.

NOTES

1. Forty participants completed the questionnaire, representing 50% of overall participants. Of the respondents, 10 were BSU students (1 undergraduate and 9 graduate); 25 taught in K-12 (1 at the elementary level, 5 at the middle school level, and 20 at the high school level), 10 taught at the college level, and 7 held administrative positions (5 in K-12, and 2 at a college). (This number comes to over 40, as some people had multiple positions: some taught at both the middle

and high school level, some were both teachers and graduate students, and some were both teachers and administrators).

2. For each response, we have provided information about the survey participant's position, when possible. If the participant simply indicated "K-12" or that they work in both middle and high schools, we have used the term "secondary school teacher."

3. At this time, states may choose between two K-12 comprehensive assessment consortia, the partnership for Assessment of Readiness for College and Careers (PARCC) (to date, adopted by 22 states and the District of Columbia) or the Smarter Balanced Assessment Consortium (to date, adopted by 25 states). (Houghton Mifflin Harcourt, 2014)

WORKS CITED

"Assessment 101: PARCC & SBAC." *Common Core*. Houghton Mifflin Harcourt, 2014. Web. 4 February 2014.

Childers, Pam, and Michael Lowry, eds. "Special Issue on Writing Across the Secondary School Curriculum." *Across the Disciplines* 9.3 (2012): n. pag. Web. 17 May 2013.

Common Core State Standards Initiative. "Standards in Your State." *Common Core State Standards Initiative: Preparing America's Students for College & Career.* 2014 Common Core State Standards Initiative, 2013. Web. 20 May 2013.

Cox, Michelle. "In Response to Today's 'Felt Need': WAC, Faculty Development, and Second Language Writers." *WAC and Second Language Writers: Research towards Linguistically and Culturally Inclusive Programs and Practices.* Eds. Terry Myers Zawacki and Michelle Cox. Fort Collins: WAC Clearinghouse and Parlor Press, 2014. 299-326. Web. 22 January 2014.

Cox, Michelle, and Ann Brunjes. "Guiding Principles for Supporting Faculty as Writers at a Teaching-Mission Institution." *Working with Faculty Writers*. Eds. Ann Ellen Geller and Michele Eodice. Boulder: Utah State UP, 2013. 191-209. Print.

Cox, Michelle, and Phyllis Gimbel. "Conversations among Teachers on Student Writing: WAC/ Secondary Education Partnerships at BSU." *Across the Disciplines* 9.3 (2012): n. pag. Web. 17 May 2013.

Guerra, Juan. "Cultivating Transcultural Citizenship: A Wtriting Across Communities Model." *Language Arts* 85.4 (2008). 296-304. *ERIC*. Web. 13 November 2014.

Kells, Michelle Hall. "Writing Across Communities: Deliberation and the Discursive Possibilities of WAC." *Reflections* 11.1 (2007): 87-108. Web. 13 November 2014.

Kerr, Clark. *The Uses of the University.* 3rd ed. Cambridge: Harvard UP, 1982. Print.

Lillge, Danielle. "Illuminating Possibilities: Secondary Writing Across the Curriculum as a Resource for Navigating Common Core State Standards." *Across the Disciplines* 9.3 (2012): n. pag. Web. 10 May 2013.

Luna, Catherine, and Cara Livingstone Turner. "The Impact of the MCAS: Teachers Talk about High-Stakes Testing." *The English Journal* 91.1 (2001): 79-87. JSTOR. Web. 22 December 2014.

National Assessment Governing Board. "Reading Framework for 2009 National Assessment of Educational Progress." Washington: U.S. Government Printing Office. 2008. Print.

Parks, Steve, and Eli Goldblatt. "Writing Beyond the Curriculum: Fostering New Collaborations in Literacy." *College English* 62.5 (2000): 584-86. JSTOR. Web. 13 November 2014.

CHAPTER 3

NEWTON'S THIRD LAW REVISITED: ACTION REACTION PAIRS IN COLLABORATION

Michael J. Lowry

> *In 1665 Cambridge University closed as precaution against an impending wave of plague. A recent graduate, Isaac Newton took time off from further study to begin understanding "the problem of motion, both heavenly and earth bound." In a particularly productive period of his life, he formalized the physics of moving objects while simultaneously inventing a new branch of mathematics (calculus) to explain motion. His famous Laws of Motion were first described in his classic text Principia Mathematica in 1687. With these generalized principles, it was possible to understand the workings of the universe. His 3rd Law explored how forces interact as pairs: a book rests on a table pushing down on the surface and the surface pushes back up on the book.*

How do WAC partnerships relate to Newton's Third Law? The idea of action/reaction may be applied to the nature of collaborative relationships in the following way: the "action" of seeking partnerships creates "reactions" often of equal (or greater) force propelling the agents in creative directions. Hansen, Hartley, Jamsen, Levin, and Nichols-Besel describe how partnerships "are sparked by curiosity, risk taking and grass roots enthusiasm" that can lead to sustainable programs in their chapter (Chapter 8). As a science educator deeply interested in using writing to promote learning, I have pondered how educators at the secondary school level could form partnerships with postsecondary institutions to improve the thinking and writing in their classroom. Like Navarro and Chion (Chapter 4), I know the value of cultivating writing skills to advance understanding within a discipline; however, as Cox and Gimbel (Chapter 2) remind us, forging collaborative communities is not limited to college-level settings. This essay will document several partnerships among secondary school educators and individuals of post-secondary institutions all in the service of improving teaching and learning.

Given the often stifling force of isolation that occurs among many teachers, the need to reach out and connect with other professionals is vital to the growth of any educator, from novice to accomplished teacher. As a physics and biology teacher at an independent day/boarding boys' school, I have felt the need to connect with other professionals who will challenge my thinking and teaching. At its most basic level, the urge to collaborate begins with an interest in improving one's craft. In July of 2011, the National Academy of Sciences released *A Framework for the Next Generation of Science Standards* (NGSS). Science educators across the country delved into the document with great interest given the implications of its content. One of the notable features of the NGSS was the inclusion of the engineering design process as part of the core practices of science (Bazerman; Giere, Bickle, and Maudlin; Petroski). It was an element unknown to many science educators and soon became an interest of mine as I reflected on how to understand this aspect of the NGSS. I needed to learn more about the subject and how it might play a role in my classroom.

One of the leaders in science and engineering design, the National Aeronautics and Space Administration (NASA) has a distinguished history of accomplishment in space and earth science, in addition to having a vibrant interest in supporting the professional growth of science educators. Part of NASA's mission is to support the recruitment of future professionals. Knowing this, I sought to partner with NASA in some way to increase my understanding of the engineering design process and advance my content understanding.

In 2012 I applied for and was accepted to a two-week workshop sponsored by NASA called the Airborne Research Experience for Educators and Students (AREES). The purpose of the program was to provide research-based experiences for middle and secondary educators through the use of the unique environment of NASA flight platforms (aircraft carrying an elaborate array of sensors). We were placed into collaborative teams and practiced science by becoming involved in NASA earth science and flight missions. In addition, these experiences were to be translated into classroom practice through the implementation of thematic curriculum modules based on a select aircraft, instrument, and research investigation. To advance our content knowledge, we attended lectures and engaged in activities from subject matter experts relevant to aircraft and research investigations. Distinguished scientists and engineers from university faculty, NASA Flight Centers, and research institutions led the lectures. Instructional content included subject matter in natural events (e.g., earthquakes, volcanoes and hurricanes), climate, remote sensing, atmospheric chemistry, and other relevant subjects. It was an intensive and exciting two-week experience throwing us into the role of student and learner.

During our second week, our hosts turned the tables on us and posed the following question: How do you bring this experience back to your classroom? It was now time for us to construct a thematic curricular unit that would span grades seven to twelve and address the content and research practices we experienced the week before. We knew that we wanted our students to experience the "doing" of science and "doing" of engineering (Schwab). In addition, we needed a topic that was sufficiently broad to allow us to generate different curricular strands. We needed to create what David Perkins of Harvard's Project Zero calls "a generative topic" (Checkley; Gardner). Because the workshop took place in California and we had taken a field trip to see the San Andreas Fault, it became clear that the study of earthquakes using airborne sensors would be a rich subject. We settled upon using a Project Based Learning (PBL) approach, posing an authentic challenge with many possible solutions. The unit needed to stretch students and challenge them to expand their Zone of Proximal Development (Vygotsky). It was important to me that writing activities would become an essential part of the unit, from writing-to-learn prompts, writing for social change challenges, and formal scientific writing assignments.

The scientists and engineers from the previous week acted as resources in their areas of content and research authenticity. Interestingly, they became fascinated with how we devised our unit and what role writing would play in it. One senior engineer asked, "Why are you incorporating all of the writing assignments? Shouldn't that happen in their English classes? I'm interested because I never really learned how to write until my first real job." They repeatedly mentioned that effective writing skills were essential to the success of scientists and engineers. Another engineer mentioned, "I learned great technical skills during my time at school; however, it was not until I came to NASA that I discovered the need to communicate my ideas and write in a persuasive way." One scientist, an editor of a major scientific journal, shared with us, "I reject many manuscripts a month not because the science is poor, but because the authors lack the ability to communicate their ideas." He stressed the importance of receiving feedback on writing; "I've learned that other eyes need to read my work before I'm ready to publish. It takes a lot of work." When we interviewed them about the kinds of writing they engaged in, we discovered a wide variety of types: research summaries, grant proposals, requests for proposals, formal technical writing, email dialogues with colleagues across the country, budget requests, and staff evaluations were some of the examples they shared. We asked about how a team of scientists would request funding to use one of NASA's aircraft for research projects, much like the one we designed in our PBL unit. They provided the template collaborative teams must submit for evaluation by the Review Committee. We used a similar template for our project: students had to describe their research project, the methods they would employ, how they would "pack the plane" with instrumentation, and also include a summary of costs. The NASA team provided access to a web-based utility that would calculate actual costs in running a mission. We strived to keep the experience as authentic as possible, including how middle and high school students used writing as a tool to advance learning. As one senior scientist mentioned of the unit we created, "I wish I had such an opportunity when I was a student."

Our collaboration with NASA created an interesting and unexpected action/reaction pair. As a participant of the workshop, I was fully prepared to expand my content knowledge of aeronautics and gain deeper insights into how NASA accomplishes its mission, "To fly what others only imagine." To my surprise and delight, I learned the engineers and scientists were interested in supporting the next generation of STEM professionals through high quality educational resources. One of the major deficits in their education was a limited ability to communicate ideas effectively. The scientists and engineers embraced the idea of fostering this skill early in school, and as a result, a WACommunity was born. The senior scientist who acts as an editor for a scientific journal began offering writing workshops for younger colleagues; he was interested in supporting the growth of his staff. Two of the engineers agreed to act as peer reviewers for my students who engaged in the curricular unit. They mentioned how they enjoyed sharing their knowledge by providing feedback to emerging scientists/engineers. One interesting interaction involved a student who was responding to a writing for social action prompt; he was composing a letter to his senator regarding the recent sequestration budget cuts. He interviewed one of the NASA engineers to learn more about how the cuts were affecting the agency and composed a convincing piece using first-hand knowledge in his letter. My students said, "It went from being a 'so what' letter to an 'ah ha' kind of thing." Just as we learned more about the work of NASA personnel, the staff at Dryden Flight Center delved into the life of educators. Newton's Third Law of action/reaction was actively at work during our summer experience.

Another collaborative experience resulting in unanticipated beneficial outcomes involves how Volunteer Professional Organizations (VPO) can support the growth and learning of secondary and postsecondary educators. For example, many such VPO's exist for educators: the National Council of Teachers of English (NCTE); the National Council of Teachers of Mathematics (NCTM); and the National Science Teachers Association (NSTA). NSTA is the largest organization dedicated to supporting the teaching and learning of science in the country. It offers many professional opportunities to its members: Professional Development Institutes, regional and national conferences and a dynamic e-professional development portal known as the Learning Center (http://learningcenter.nsta.org/).

Teachers may also volunteer to serve on committees with various purposes. I was appointed to one such committee, the Children's Book Council Review Panel, whose purpose is to evaluate all new science trade books for a particular year. With over 150 books published any given year, the committee's task is to select twenty to thirty exemplary texts that meet committee standards for excellence. Rubrics include criteria such as the accuracy of the science described, age appropriateness of topics, and the variety of cultures represented in the books. In particular, research indicated that few children of color see themselves portrayed as "scientific," so the committee has been interested in identifying texts that speak to that audience in compelling ways. After I had volunteered for this committee, I learned how to evaluate the reading level of a book and how important the interplay between written text and effective visuals can be when explaining complex scientific phenomena. One member of our committee, a professor of education and a reading specialist, challenged us "to do more than just review the books." She wanted us to use them and create assessments to strengthen students' cognitive development. Long before the Common Core's emphasis on using non-fiction texts to advance learning, our committee settled upon using these books to support literacy and language development along with promoting science understanding. Science teachers at all levels benefit from the reviews and use them to spur learning within the discipline.

One early collaboration that resulted from my work on the review panel centered on the annotated bibliography we created for the Outstanding Trade Books in Science. The short synopsis, along with a brief commentary of what made the book exemplary, was an excellent exercise in concise writing. Hansen et al. describe how curiosity can spark a vital collaboration (Chapter 8). I was talking with a colleague who mentioned how he was looking for a way to use writing in his classroom. I suggested we use the trade books in some way. The director of our writing center (who was my team teaching partner) suggested we review science books and write our own summaries in the style of the committee. After reading a book, the sixth graders drafted summaries and then met with our twelfth-grade students, who were trained about how to offer supportive feedback to young writers. The sixth-grade students began to master the art of revising their work to more effectively communicate their ideas. We assembled their final drafts into an annotated bibliography, which the middle school librarian used as a resource for all students. Twelfth-grade students acted as peer tutors to the sixth graders, and the librarian and writing center director assisted in compiling the final bibliographies. The bibliographies expanded in size and purpose, morphing into what Margaretha Ebbers refers to as a text set (41). These collections of different genres of books (fiction, non-fiction, biographies, field guides, and reference materials) present scientific information in different ways.

Collections of these text sets can be used to support inquiry-based instruction in science by supporting students as they pose questions, design investigations, and confirm and expand the knowledge they have learned through direct investigations. In their book *Inquiring Scientist, Inquiring Readers: Using Nonfiction to Promote Science Literacy*, Jessica Fries-Gaith and Terry Shiverdecker bring this concept to fruition; they weave together best practices for science and literacy instruction in a way that makes sense for the classroom. What began as a simple act of working on a review panel created an equal and opposite reaction rich with collaboration that spawned a host of writing, thinking and learning among young learners. I shared the assignment with the chair of our committee, and she used it as the inspiration for a unit with her university pre-service science teachers. It has become a favorite of her students, because they learn science content while reading the books, and they explore how to use the books with writing assignments in their classrooms. The "reaction" of my committee service lives on in the work of these pre-service teachers.

The previous examples demonstrate how action/reaction pairs between collaborators advance the professional growth of educators in oblique ways. Can the act of writing itself spark direct growth for educators? In other words, can we apply the principles of the writing process to advance the development of educators? And what role does collaboration play in the development process? I explored those questions as I embarked on the long and arduous process of seeking National Board Certification. Modeled after the bar examination that is used to determine if a candidate is qualified to practice law in a given state, the National Board for Professional Teaching Standards (NBPTS) seeks to identify what a teacher should know and be able to do as an accomplished teacher. The originators of NBPTS, a group of outstanding postsecondary educators across disciplines, has identified five core propositions related to what a teacher should know and be able to do:

1. Teachers are committed to students and their learning.
2. Teachers know the subjects they teach and how to teach those subjects to students.
3. Teachers are responsible for managing and monitoring student learning.
4. Teachers think systematically about their practice and learn from experience.
5. Teachers are members of learning communities.

The assessment process requires candidates to complete two major components: a portfolio of classroom practice, including samples of student work and video recordings of instruction, and a content knowledge assessment administered at a testing center. At the core of the process is writing: writing about practice; writing about assessment; writing about student growth and personal growth; and reflecting on how to improve as a professional. I was deeply engaged in the writing process while examining my work as an educator: prewriting (inventing approaches and aspects of learning to review); carefully responding to the prompts with supporting evidence; outlining my ideas with a narrative structure; proofreading; seeking outside feedback; and rewriting and revising my drafts. I was engaged in this iterative loop for a year as I put my practice "under the microscope" of review and self-reflection. The action of writing created an equal and opposite force that transformed how I think about teaching and learning: I no longer just "blazed through" a class, a unit, a semester; the writing process caused me to continuously question and reflect on what made my actions effective. Ultimately, I was successful in obtaining certification due largely to applying the writing process to my work. I joined a group sponsored by the national board to act as mentors to aspiring candidates. I found that mentoring a colleague was as valuable as going through the process itself.

Mary Sandowski, a biology teacher from Seattle, and I attended a dynamic Professional Development workshop that took place at the Olympic Park Institute outside the Olympic National Park in Washington. We were learning about the ecology of old growth forests of the Pacific Northwest. While crawling over the massive remains of fallen spruce, Mary mentioned that she was interested in attempting National Board Certification. I encouraged her to start the process and offered to be a mentor as she moved through the long journey of completing its requirements. Over the course of a year, we began a dialog that was highly rewarding to both of us: she would forward drafts of reflective writing about various submissions and I would offer feedback to her ideas. An interesting pattern emerged in our dialog: she would make claims about "student understanding being advanced" and I would respond "where's the evidence?" Before long, Mary realized she needed to offer support for any claims; more importantly, she began to question why she was doing certain actions with her students and how that supported their learning. The "magic" of self-reflection was beginning to take hold of Mary: "I never realized how slowing down to reflect on my work in writing would act as the catalyst for change. We are so focused on moving forward, that we forget to look back." Mary was grasping what Navarro and Chion mention in their chapter, that covering a syllabus does not guarantee deep learning (Chapter 4). Writing becomes the vehicle that "slows us down" and invites discourse about our practice as educators. I suggested she might try a writing-to-learn activity to begin a unit and track student comprehension by using a portfolio system. She instituted the idea, and it became a valuable assessment "artifact" for her certification process. Mary revised her essays multiple times, demonstrating clearer insight into the work of her students and her role in supporting their growth with each version. My "action" with Mary caused an equal "reaction" in my own practice: was I practicing what I preached when it came to using writing in my classroom? My dialog with Mary forced me to reevaluate how I use writing and prompted me to take new directions in how I use this tool with my students. I created an assignment having students delve into scientific literature and write concise summaries of that literature. It is an assignment that continues to pay dividends with learning today; students mention in summative assessments that the research summaries forced them to become more effective communicators. The writing process as practiced by student and educator alike became the vehicle for professional and personal growth, and this insight sprang from my collaboration with the National Board for Professional Teaching Standards.

Over 350 years ago, Newton created a framework for understanding how actions of "unlike bodies may interact to move in understandable ways" (Westfall 105). He most likely never imagined his Laws of Motion might extend to collaborative "action/reaction" pairs; nonetheless the genius of his ideas lies in their applicability to other fields. My own collaborations have challenged me to move outside my classroom and interact with "unlike bodies," with educators in different fields and at other academic levels. By taking the risk of moving outside of the familiar, I have been rewarded with profound professional growth. Whether it is forming partnerships through the National Writing Project, IWCA, WAC, or working closely with a colleague to support writing, thinking and learning, these partnerships are crucial hallmarks of professional practice.

WORKS CITED

Bazerman, Charles. *Shaping Written Knowledge*. Madison: U of Wisconsin P, 1988. Print.

Checkley, Kathy. "The First Seven ... and the Eighth: A Conversation with Howard Gardner." *Educational Leadership* 55 (1997): 8-13. Web. 13 November 2014.

Ebbers, Margaretha. "Science Text Sets: Using Various Genres to Promote Literacy and Inquiry." *Language Arts* 80 (2002): 40-50. Web. 13 November 2014.

Gardner, Howard. *Frames of Mind: The Theory of Multiple Intelligences*. New York: Basic Books, 1983. Print.

Giere, Ronald N., John Bickle, and Robert Maudlin. *Understanding Scientific Reasoning*. Belmont: Thomson Wadsworth, 2006. Print.

Fries-Gaith, Jessica, and Terry Shiverdecker. *Inquiring Scientist, Inquiring Readers: Using Nonfiction to Promote Science Literacy*. Arlington: NSTA Press, 2012. Print.

Petroski, Henry. *Engineering by Design: How Engineers Get from Thought to Thing.* Cambridge: Harvard UP, 1996. Print.

Schwab, Joseph Jackson. *The Teaching of Science as Enquiry.* Cambridge: Harvard UP. 1962. Print.

Sylvester, R., and W. Greenidge. "Digital Storytelling: Extending the Potential for Struggling Writers." *The Reading Teacher* 63.4 (2009): 284-95. Web.

Vygotsky, Lev S. *Mind in Society.* Cambridge: Harvard UP, 1978. Print.

Westfall, Richard S. *Never at Rest: A Biography of Isaac Newton.* Cambridge: Cambridge UP, 1983. Print.

CHAPTER 4

SHAPING DISCIPLINARY DISCOURSES IN HIGH SCHOOL: A TWO-WAY COLLABORATIVE WRITING PROGRAM

Federico Navarro and Andrea Revel Chion

We work in university, high school, and teacher training courses in different disciplines (applied linguistics and didactics of biology) in Argentina. We share an interest in the discursive and epistemic singularity of school writing within the framework of various subjects, and in that regard, we both acknowledge—and worry about—the rare, specific instances in which they are taught. We are motivated by our intention to prompt teachers' and students' reflection on the fact that writing stimulates thinking, generates and fosters learning, and has inherent features that must be mastered before participating in any classroom discussion and training.

It is against this backdrop that the School Writing Program[1] was formulated as a subject compulsorily taken in the school where the program was implemented,[2] although it has not been formally introduced into the high school curriculum nationwide. It is taught by a writing teacher and articulated with various curriculum subjects on a rotating basis throughout each school year. Students read and write based on relevant epistemological frameworks, themes, corpora, reading assignments, and linguistic dimensions that are agreed upon by the writing teacher and the subject teacher. This proposal is unprecedented in Argentine high schools' curricula, which are compartmentalized into areas, except for a few pilot or short-term projects. Besides, some recent interesting proposals have focused alternatively on the linguistic specificity of school writing practices (Desinano; Di Stefano, Rizzi, and Axeruld) or on their epistemological specificity (Carlino), but they do not elaborate sufficiently on the articulation of both aspects.

The proposal to create a specific setting for writing-in-the-disciplines was welcomed enthusiastically by officials and colleagues when it was outlined in 2011, and gradually extended to the school curriculum in 2013 to become a required course taught to first graders (12-13-year-olds), second graders (13-14-year-olds), and fourth graders (15-16-year-olds). Likewise, students gradually overcame their initial distrust of a writing-oriented subject that articulates various areas.

Usually, educators claim that this type of project is too time-consuming and thus prevents teachers from covering their syllabi, but it is equally true that an unconnected heap of knowledge and the completion of syllabi do not guarantee students' understanding, applicability, and transferability of this knowledge. Completed syllabi, but inert knowledge? We do not think that is acceptable.

Some educators also frequently assert that subject teachers do not know how to teach the special features of writing, but this is no less true than the fact that language teachers do not know the special features of writing vis-à-vis school subjects. It follows that collaborative work is the most viable alternative in order to incorporate writing into each subject. The program described below is intended to show a possible path to solve these concerns.

TEACHING WRITING IN SCHOOL

There is consensus about the need for students to know and identify the meanings of natural sciences, social sciences, and the humanities. Thus, students should be able to master their "languages" so that the gap between them and their teachers will narrow, and the communication between them will become more fluent.

It should be pointed out that, for the most part, subject teachers need appropriate and specific linguistic and didactic tools to perform explicit and productive work with their students' reading and writing practices. That is, training in the didactics of writing-in-the-disciplines is necessary to identify the dimensions of language involved in the production of written material, to use a meta-language to direct the work, and to structure the development processes of the more complex writing practices. In line with this, language teachers need training and specialization in the various conceptual frameworks and rhetorical styles of the specific disciplinary cultures. As a result, the exchange and the symmetrical two-way collaboration between writing teachers and subject teachers serve as the starting point for a comprehensive approach to reading and writing.

School and academic reading and writing practices at the different levels and in the different subjects are new practices that must be taught, explored, and exercised (Carlino; Kelly and Bazerman; Rivard and Straw). Put another way, they are not natural skills or skills acquired only during elementary education.

Teaching the specificity of school writing and the specificity of disciplinary discourse are two closely related aspects. In other words, some relevant aspects of school writing are inextricably related to the rhetorical and epistemological specificities of certain fields, while other fields can be generalized, to a lesser or greater degree, in school writing. Partnerships among secondary and university educators are important to improve student learning. The contents and competences addressed by the School Writing Program explore these two dimensions, as explained later on.

Besides, teaching contents *through* language and teaching *about* language are two sides of the same coin. While reading and writing enable one to gain disciplinary knowledge, it should not be overlooked that disciplinary knowledge is written and negotiated in the classroom from certain specific linguistic practices and dimensions, which must be taught and learned (Rose and Martin 18). We believe that the power of writing as an epistemic practice is associated with its power as a rhetorical practice.

Determining the importance of the reading and writing work in all school subjects falls within the scope of the need to deal with the *hidden curriculum* (Jackson). In particular, students have a given cultural capital (Bourdieu; Ezcurra) that comprises cognitive skills (analyzing, summarizing, relating, judging, and applying information), critical academic habits (using the dictionary, making a documentary search, taking notes, reading graphs and charts, synthesizing information, using information and communication technology tools), metacognitive and self-regulatory skills (monitoring learning, identifying weaknesses and strengths of their own learning, spotting and fixing mistakes, and organizing time), and information, concepts, and thinking frameworks. Within these components of cultural capital, discipline writing practices play a key role. Unless students develop literacy practices by reflecting upon and explicitly exercising the articulation between linguistic and epistemic dimensions under certain guidelines, too much reliance will be placed on the competences acquired by them in their cultural and family settings, i.e., on their cultural capital.

A WRITING PROGRAM FOR THE SCHOOL CURRICULUM

The School Writing Program might be thought of as a special setting of biology, civics, or math—or any other subject—where written communicative competence is exercised, or as a subject of reading and writing that borrows contents, epistemic practices, and materials from other subjects of the same school grade. In fact, it is a combination of both.

Although the program has its own space in the curriculum, it is articulated reciprocally with other subjects according to negotiated dynamics that depend on the participating teachers of secondary levels. It is a subject that does not revolve around reading and writing exercises isolated from the students' curriculum-related needs and specificities, nor is it limited to surmounting the reading and writing difficulties not dealt with by traditional subjects.

Also, one of the goals of the program is to agree on collaborative didactic interventions with teachers from different areas and subjects. This aspect centers on the articulation between reading and writing practices and the rhetorical and epistemic specificity of the various areas of the school curriculum. On top of that, this articulation implies a true process of interdisciplinary teacher training. In this way, collaborative work between writing teachers and subject teachers starts a two-way original training process for the school dynamics, where the fragmentation of teacher training, subjects, and teacher practice is currently the norm. This cross-institutional training and collaboration among educators is especially enriching, because it originated at the actual teaching site, so it makes full sense to all participants.

From the students' point of view, the program affords an opportunity to further their school writing practices by addressing specific needs arising from their subjects, to become meta-linguistically aware, and to acquire an operating meta-language that enables them to revise and improve their written work on their own, and to recognize the role of reading and writing as fundamental practices for their performance in the specific school subjects. This work is not intended only for a higher degree of adaptation to school literacy practices, but also for the development of a fundamental strategy to better learn the contents of the subject syllabi.

From the subject teachers' standpoint, the program is an opportunity to reflect upon, modify, and state expressly the role of literacy practices in their subjects through the development of specific tools and goals in cooperation with the writing teachers. In addition, writing teachers can boost their work with written language in school by incorporating materials and knowledge from other areas.

The design of the program comprises its own space in the curriculum through a weekly, eighty-minute class within the regular school schedule that is like any other required subject. It is taught by a writing teacher that works in coordination with teachers of different subjects. Every trimester, the writing course is articulated with a different subject and teacher. In its first year (2011), the program was implemented in fourth grade (15-16-year-old students), and writing teachers worked with history, biology, and physics teachers. In its second year (2012), the program was extended to first-grade courses (12-13-year-old students) and included math, civics, and geography teachers. In its third year (2013), second-grade courses (13-14-year-old students) were added and some courses and teachers remained on the program (math and geography), while others joined the program (biology). Therefore, a high school freshman would participate in the program for three years. The program intends to be introduced into every grade of the school curriculum, because each stage has needs and goals related to literacy practices that must be recognized and institutionalized by the school.

Every trimester, students work on reading material, speech genres, authors, theoretical contents and frameworks, and communicative needs of a subject that they are taking simultaneously. If this proposal surprises teachers and officials alike, it also comes as a surprise to students: A subject that is history, but it's not history? Why is my writing on biology evaluated if I'm not being taught biology? Why are teachers of different subjects teaching the same topic? Part of the challenge posed to the teacher in charge of the course is to transform students' representations of the organization, teaching, learning, and evaluation of the curriculum, areas, and subjects, by showing them the epistemic value of writing.

The collaboration with each subject teacher cannot be reduced to only one trimester in a given year or a span of several years. The plan is designed to last about two years, and then rotate to new teachers. Thus, an attempt is made to largely impact the teaching community. Collaborative work is assumed to be a training process that requires a minimum period to mature and settle. Afterwards, when participants develop independent strategies to teach writing, the work with disciplinary rhetorical practices must go necessarily from the writing classroom to writing in the classroom. This means that the collaboration is no longer needed. The rotating nature of the program is one of its most remarkable strengths: it enables interested teachers to participate, sparks others' curiosity, allows dissatisfied teachers to leave the program in an orderly fashion, and permits those who are not so sure about participating to wait for the right time to join in.

However, as the Writing Program aims to tackle specific communication challenges within the content subjects and engage teachers into a training process, the decision on which teachers continue, join, or leave the program is not only personal, but also, and essentially, institutional. Most teachers in the school did volunteer to participate, and there is actually a waiting list of teachers willing to take part in the program. Some of these teachers only teach at the secondary level, while others simultaneously teach at postsecondary and university levels, and most of them usually engage in all kinds of educational projects. On the whole, participating teachers are open to new, exciting educational scenarios, so gathering colleagues' interest has never been an issue. After three years running, the impact of the program on students' literacies as perceived by teachers has definitely reinforced that initial interest.

In addition, the flexible nature of the curricula organization in Argentina leaves room for this kind of reform program and allows for bottom-up changes. Secondary teachers in Argentina are, in general, free to choose or even design their own coursebooks. They can usually include what they consider relevant contents for their specific students and their academic, institutional, and sociocultural context. This means that innovative, enthusiastic institutions can foster different kinds of projects and programs on their own without being constrained by school districts' policies. As a matter of fact, many districts' reports and syllabi do encourage writing across the curriculum initiatives (Ministerio de Educación), although this does not necessarily imply the implementation of actual writing programs.

COLLABORATING TO TEACH, EVALUATE, AND INNOVATE

The negotiated collaboration dynamics are a key feature of the program. This collaboration is neither isolated nor focused on the beginning of the school year. On the contrary, writing teachers and subject teachers must, to a lesser or greater degree, negotiate throughout the collaboration period. This creates a setting for educational projects and innovation that, despite the extra effort required, proves very encouraging for its participants. Before the beginning of the collaboration period, participating teachers define several aspects, such as the disciplinary texts to be used, the evaluation criteria to be followed, and mainly, the reading and writing practices and dimensions that will be addressed. These practices and dimensions are directly related to the aspects proper to the reading and writing practices of the subject, the discipline, and the school. During the trimester, teachers are in contact with one another over the phone, by email, and in person to discuss the development and implementation of the activities planned, apart from any new initiatives. At the end of the trimester, teachers meet to evaluate the implementation of the collaboration, agree on the students' final grades, and plan any changes to the following year's collaboration.

The common grade is also awarded jointly by the writing teacher and the subject teacher at the end of the trimester; every student's homework, coursework, and exam grades in both areas are compared, and a final, common grade is agreed on. This innovative feature derives from the need for students to commit themselves to take part in a demanding, complex subject, which nonetheless is not part of the curriculum, strictly speaking. Yet, it has a less expected effect: it helps consolidate the proposal with the students because of the ties between epistemic frameworks and writing practices, one of the premises of the program, and translate into an aspect as significant as the trimester grade.

Also open to intense negotiation is the evaluation method. The most conventional method of evaluation is an exam integrating reading and writing skills that tests the topics dealt with throughout the trimester in practice. Albeit integrating topics and texts of the specific subject, this exam is graded by the writing teacher and is considered to belong to the writing course. Furthermore, written assignments and participation in classroom discussions and activities throughout the trimester are also assessed. Another method of evaluation involves incorporating reading and writing dimensions into exams explicitly, and homework assignments of the subject articulated with the program. In this case, the subject teacher, the writing teacher, or both, grade the students' written work, and a final grade is awarded in light of the students' literacy practices.

The subject is not part of the mandatory contents of the school curriculum, at least for the time being. The introduction of this device into the school schedule like any other subject enables administrators, faculty, students and parents to envision that, in the future and upon making any modification suggested by experience, it may become a curricular subject in high school.

WHAT TO WRITE IN SCHOOL

A didactic proposal to teach and learn to write must primarily define the specific writing aspects to be explored in the classroom, and how they will be explored. It becomes necessary to determine the language and writing theory to be used, the aspects of such theory selected for teaching, and how they will be taught. This represents one of the biggest challenges presented by the School Writing Program, because language deeply influences us in our capacity as social subjects in that it plays an essential role in the construction of our identities.

Language in general and writing in particular are usually regarded as a single skill that cannot be segmented into specific and differentiated practices, dimensions, and resources. Further, writing is often related exclusively to important but insufficient aspects, such as spelling rules or correctness criteria applied regardless of use, and its varying degrees of adequacy. Similarly, language tends to be considered a natural object that may be addressed alternatively by one or another linguistic theory without any consequence.

But this is not the case at all. There are cognitive, formalist, functionalist, and pragmatic linguistic theories, among others, and each results in language and writing configurations that are very different from one another. School and academic writing cannot be taught with a linguistic conception arising from common sense or with outdated grammars, or dictionaries that disregard the scientific advances of the past decades. This does not mean that subject teachers must be experts in linguistics before explicitly incorporating reading and writing, but they do need to receive some training on these subjects and on collaborative projects. In addition, teachers can take advantage of students' conceptions of language and writing to enhance classroom work.

The aspects addressed in the School Writing Program fall into five broad dimensions: basic literacy competences; cognitive and linguistic meta-competences; school speech genres; information and communication technologies (ICTs);

and rules. These dimensions are explored below, pointing out some specific matters taken up with 15- and 16-year-old students.

The general methodology that relates the aspects tackled in class focuses on the *transformation* of texts according to detailed guidelines that draw distinctions between the various dimensions. Accordingly, students must syntactically rearrange an excerpt without modifying the meaning or the lexicon, adapt the lexicon to different readerships, change the punctuation of a paragraph to make it clearer, reorganize the position and articulation of an authoritative quote in a reading report, or enlarge the space between paragraphs without modifying the space between lines, among many other possible transformations. In turn, this methodology explores ludic aspects, such as the generation of mockery, and uses non-academic communicative practices familiar to students, like a detailed analysis of non-school unwritten speech genres. Students follow a basic series of steps: first, they (individually, in pairs, or the entire class) read and deconstruct others' texts (materials of the area, other students' texts); then, they (individually and in pairs) do their own writing based on previously discussed issues; finally, they read and rewrite those texts, and the process starts again. Providing settings to rewrite texts is remarkably enriching, because it reinforces the representation of writing as a complex rhetorical process by stages and with multiple dimensions. At the same time, students have an opportunity to devise strategies to deconstruct, rephrase, and adapt their own and others' written work. In sum, texts are not only written, but also summarized, evaluated, reinforced, mocked, quoted, etc., because mature writing is, in reality, permanent rewriting where texts and contents are adapted and modified. (Alvarado 47)

BASIC LITERACY COMPETENCES

The program intends for students to develop basic literacy competences applicable to all school writing practices, but that can also become more specific in each subject. These general linguistic competencies include: explaining, describing, narrating, organizing paragraphs, summarizing, quoting, adapting, expressly stating, depersonalizing, nominalizing, rephrasing, hedging, boosting, etc. To a lesser or greater degree, these aspects should be covered by practically every school and academic writing course, although the particular features of the respective disciplines may require prioritizing certain writing practices over others. For example, even though any scientific discipline must quote previous sources, and the strategies and rules to quote and use a bibliography vary from discipline to discipline.

To illustrate our point, we will refer to the work on hedging and boosting articulated with history. In the introduction and conclusion of a research article published in a scientific journal and used as required reading in the subject, the authors identify resources to hedge and boost. These resources are crucial in scientific-academic discourse, not least in the humanities, such as history (Hyland 57-58), because new contributions must be fitted into the body of knowledge already accepted by the community and, at the same time, must not constitute a threat to that community (hedging). With that in mind, those contributions must be put forward with enough commitment and conviction to be taken into account (boosting). That is, the degree of certainty and accuracy of the assertions does not only depend on how sure we are of those assertions, but also on a correlation of forces in the socially situated production of discourses (Myers). This double articulation that embraces the key assertions in scientific-academic discourse is also relevant when a student presents and defends his positions before an expert teacher. Thus, the work with hedges and boosters triggers the discussion about the socio-historically specific ways of negotiating and validating scientific knowledge between writers and readers. Aside from that, the different parts of the genre are related to the precedence of hedging (in the introduction) or boosting (in the conclusion). The excerpts analyzed are rephrased afterwards by incorporating excessive hedges and boosters to mock the original text. These games enable students to reflect on the features that make a school text adequate or inadequate, and also promote students' creativity and interest.

COGNITIVE AND LINGUISTIC META-COMPETENCES

The development and consolidation of cognitive and linguistic meta-competences might help students adopt a critical attitude towards their own and others' reading and writing practices and acquire an analysis meta-language. This dimension enables them to attain a theoretical and reflexive balance in a predominantly practical pedagogical approach to writing. Meta-competences make exercises more meaningful, prompt discussions about and the rearrangement of prior conceptions of the development of writing competences, as well as enable students to become more autonomous and to gain critical insights as far as their writing is concerned. Additionally, meta-competences can help foster students' involvement in the subject and increase their interest. Their reading and writing backgrounds are reflected upon; mistakes in their written work and in others' are spotted and corrected; the functional varieties of language are analyzed in view of political, geographical, social, and situational dimensions; the mass media discourse (nationwide newspapers) is deconstructed; paragraphs are read and annotated; and the subjective and objective dimensions of scientific-academic discourse are discussed among students and teachers.

With respect to the latter aspect, in articulation with physics, the allegedly objective and impersonal nature of scientific-academic discourse is discussed analyzing some depersonalization strategies on which that construction is based (García Negroni), including: nominalization (which eliminates the participants' roles), metonymy (where an inanimate element, like "the book" or "the theory," is an agent), passive voice (which might eliminate the agent), non-finite verb forms (which provide no morphological information on person and number), and the first person plural (which conceals the individuality of a single speaker). Students work with biographical texts of a key author read in physics (Stephen Hawking) and play at depersonalizing them, thus showing the artificiality of the mechanism.

The articulation with biology introduces language functional varieties associated with contextual factors: national languages (geographical and political variations: Argentina's language, Spain's language), sociolects (social variations according to the speakers' age, ethnic group, profession, sex, etc.; teenagers' language, lawyers' language), genres and registers (cultural and situational variations), and idiolects (individual variations). Videos from series, movies, and TV programs are used to recognize varieties, and dichotomies are discussed that may arouse students' intense interest, such as correct/adequate and homogeneity/heterogeneity. This reflection enables students to elaborate on the explanatory sequence in biology (Revel Chion), described as a key feature in the discourse of that field. The exercises entail rewriting a biology explanation in a specific social language (and a specific situational context).

SCHOOL SPEECH GENRES

The program deals with school speech genres that are closely related to the respective disciplines and relevant to the students' particular writing practices: a comprehensive history exam; an explanation of a topic in biology; a newspaper editorial; and a reading report in physics. The genres selected are practiced and requested in reading and writing assignments in the subjects articulated with the program. This reinforces the collaborative dynamics and makes coursework meaningful.

The work on speech genres is carried out according to three sets of features used to describe them (Bakhtin). First, their circulation: typical speaker(s), recipient(s), and situational and social contexts. Second, their socio-discursive goals: the purpose and social role of the genres. Third, their textualization: the issues addressed and the typical grammatical and lexical resources presented by the genres, as well as their structures.

The articulation with history is aimed at deconstructing, in detail, the comprehensive exam genre, which students write for the first time during this period based on real samples from previous years. They identify their readers' expectations and goals, and some typical features of its textualization. The tasks requested in the assignments are thoroughly analyzed: the aspects that must be mandatorily included in the answer, the aspects that are taken for granted but must be accounted for anyway, the key words of the assignment that must be used in the answer, and how much time will be used in each answer. Because teachers usually request narrative, explanatory, and descriptive texts, they are distinguished from one another and described. The writing activity is the preparation of the tasks of a comprehensive history exam based on a source text in which students act as the teacher. The degree of difficulty and explicitness of the assignment is proportionately adjusted.

INFORMATION AND COMMUNICATION TECHNOLOGIES

Information and communication technologies (ICTs) influence every contemporary school writing practice, and accordingly, it is our intention to include them in the program. The objective is to make more extensive use of practices familiar to and used by students in school and university, other than for social or recreational purposes. Students discuss strategies to assess the adequacy, relevance, and usefulness of online sources found on Google in school; specify the features of an email account for sending school homework; and explore the use of the word processor to do school writing.

In connection with this aspect, one class focuses on a discussion of format. Students pursue at least three goals: exploring IT tools with which students are not fully familiar (such as paragraph breaks), placing emphasis on important aspects (like justifying a text), and proposing formal features (e.g., font type and size) to practice adapting texts to them. It is a practical approach through the use of netbooks in class, as students must turn a text without a given format into one with the format required.

RULES

Although it is reductionist to consider rules to be the fundamental aspect taught by school in reference to writing, they permeate school education and, for that reason, the program emphasizes and systematizes them. The program also deals with punctuation and accentuation. Instead of going over innumerable rules, teachers employ a mainly practical approach, exploring and practicing useful general principles and rewriting texts with mistakes. The primary goal is to underscore the importance of monitoring one's own accentuation and punctuation. Also, teachers examine quotation rules, because they are new to most students and proper to academic and school discourse. In class, they analyze relevant general data, namely author, title, and date, as well as the specific rules for some disciplines.

EVALUATING TO IMPROVE

The School Writing Program has already been consolidated after having been implemented and adjusted in three grades of the curriculum (first, second, and fourth), including the preparation of the first didactic materials in the form of booklets, with the school officials' permanent support, and the participation of more subject teachers.

In the classroom, students first focused on the (in)validity and (in)viability of the course during its first year of implementation, but afterwards they were concerned with specific and useful issues, such as the aspects to be practiced and the subjects with which to articulate the program. In fact, an anonymous survey of students conducted at the end of the 2012 school year revealed that 80% found the program useful to a lesser or greater extent, and 42% found it quite or extremely useful. The importance of this information lies in the fact that it is the students' subjective, anonymous insight regarding an unprecedented demanding course. The survey also showed high heterogeneity on the issues that students had found most and least useful. This means that, through their opinions, they showed that their perceptions on their writing strengths and weaknesses are wholly dissimilar.

In respect to grades, about half of the students earned similar grades in the participating subject and in the writing course. This general tendency is interesting, because it shows that, broadly speaking, the articulation between the Writing Program and the subjects translates into a relatively high degree of consistency of the students' performance in the areas articulated. From the rest of the students, about half attained a higher grade in the writing course, and therefore raised their subject final grades and, conversely, those who received a lower grade in the writing course consequently had lower final subject grades.

The program made a substantial impact on students' literacy practices, bringing back and consolidating previous rhetorical practices and, above all, incorporating, developing, and making explicit new rhetorical competences.

Furthermore, the program was embraced readily by participating teachers, which was evidenced in the year-end self-assessments and in the teachers' workshops, which actually led to the collective decision for teachers to continue participating. Apart from that, the program made a profound impact on participating teachers' reading and writing didactic practices. The physics teacher made the reading report assignments more complex, modified them, and expressly requested that the answers indicate the strategies to quote, depersonalize, and argue that were practiced in the Writing Program, which were then assessed. The history teacher incorporated exam feedback based on collective rephrasing exercises.

For writing teachers, permanent collaboration with teachers of the other subjects enabled them to understand some specific features of the discipline's discourse, such as the importance of distinguishing social groups and their conflicting interests in the explanations of the history class.

We believe there are five reasons why other schools might implement their own School Writing Programs: (1) Argentine high schools usually have teachers eager to innovate in their practices and officials looking forward to implementing policies that systematize the ties between the curriculum and the occasional or isolated precedents that address school writing; (2) this program responds to education agencies' demands, both because it works on the reading and writing of discipline-specific texts and contents, and because it counters problems repeatedly diagnosed by general tests on school literacy competences; (3) this program has solid theoretical and empirical foundations arising from updated literature on the issue, because the program is a critical adaptation of the Writing Across the Curriculum proposal, combining discipline-specific competences and courses with competences and courses related to school reading and writing needs; (4) the logistic design of the program makes it intrinsically elastic, which enables schools to adjust it to various institutional and teaching frameworks; and (5) the program gives leeway to experiment and to discover the needs to be addressed.

CONCLUSIONS

The School Writing Program seems to be making a huge impact on students' literacy practices, on their perceptions and acceptance of the initiative, and on participating teachers' didactic practices. The differentiated ludic work performed, under certain guidelines, on dimensions and aspects proper to writing assists in the training of writers that plan and monitor their work, rewrite and modify their drafts, and use speech genres and resources adequate for their purposes and readerships. Thus, the program explicitly incorporates into the school curriculum a set of communicative competences that are essential, but are generally invisible or unsystematically taught; at the same time, students learn these competences in conjunction with diverse subjects and areas. The School Writing Program, thanks to its collaborative and rotating design, intends to put the work on these competences on the institutional and didactic agenda. The ultimate goal is for these competences to be incorporated into the various subjects' syllabi and taught by the subject teachers that participated in this training initiative or in other similar ones. Hence, the program is intended to produce effects on teachers' training so that it will not only improve their practice, but it will also lead them to apply this proposal to other teaching settings with their colleagues.

Learning school literacy practices is not a moral "duty" of students or an element we believe indispensable for an ideal school. Rather, it is what teachers, institutions, and curricula actually expect and assess of students. Said another way, students who do not succeed or who are unable to communicate through the literacy practices expected are unlikely to finish high school or to satisfactorily do so. This is because the irregular or incomplete management of the reading and writing practices of school and the curriculum disciplines limits students' access to the subjects' forms of reasoning, and bars them from joining a learning community that requires recognizable communicative competences.

NOTES

1. This device was discussed in prior research (Navarro; Navarro and Revel Chion).
2. The project described in this book was implemented in Colegio de la Ciudad, a private school located in the City of Buenos Aires, Argentina.

WORKS CITED

Alvarado, Maite. "Enfoques en la enseñanza de la escritura." *Entre líneas. Teorías y enfoques en la enseñanza de la escritura, la gramática y la literatura.* Ed. Maite Alvarado. Buenos Aires: Manantial, 2001. 13-51. Print.

Bakhtin, Mikhail. "El problema de los géneros discursivos." *Estética de la creación verbal.* Buenos Aires: Siglo XXI Editores, 2005. 248-93. Print.

Bourdieu, Pierre. *Capital Cultural, Escuela y Espacio Social.* Mexico: Siglo XXI Editores, 1997. Print.

Carlino, P. "Escribir y leer en la universidad: responsabilidad compartida entre alumnos, docentes e instituciones." *Leer y escribir en la universidad.* Ed. P. Carlino. Buenos Aires: Lectura y Vida, International Reading Association, 2004. 5-21. Print.

Carlino, Paula, and Silvia Martínez, eds. *Lectura y escritura, un asunto de todos.* Neuquén: Universidad Nacional del Comahue, 2009. Print.

Desinano, Norma, ed. *Crónica de una experiencia en la Escuela Media. Proyecto integral de lectura y escritura.* Rosario: Laborde Editor, 2007. Print.

Di Stefano, Marina, Rizzi, Laura, and Axelrud, Brenda. "Didáctica de la lectura y la escritura desde disciplinas diversas de la escuela media. Una experiencia en escuelas con población vulnerable de la Ciudad de Buenos Aires." *Universidad Nacional de Catamarca–UNESCO Chair on Reading and Writing, San Fernando del Valle de Catamarca, II Reading and Writing Conference [Jornadas de Lectura y Escritura]*, 28-30 June 2006.

Ezcurra, Ana María. "Abandono estudiantil en educación superior. Hipótesis y conceptos." *Admisión a la universidad y selectividad social. Cuando la democratización es más que un problema de "ingresos."* Ed. N. Gluz. Los Polvorines: Universidad Nacional de General Sarmiento, (2011). 23-62. Print.

García, Negroni, and María Marta. "Subjetividad y discurso científico-académico. Acerca de algunas manifestaciones de la subjetividad en el artículo de investigación en español." *Signos* 41.66 (2008): 5-31. Print.

Hyland, Ken. *Metadiscourse: Exploring Interaction in Writing*. London: Continuum, 2005. Print.

Jackson, Philip. *La vida en las aulas*. 6th ed. Madrid: Morata, 2001. Print.

Kelly, Gregory K., and Charles Bazerman. "How Students Argue Scientific Claims. A Rhetorical- Semantic Analysis." *Applied Linguistics* 24.1. (2003): 28-55. USA: Oxford UP.

Lemke, Jay. *Aprender a hablar ciencia. Lenguaje, aprendizaje y valores*. Barcelona: Paidós, 1997. Print.

Ministerio de Educación del Gobierno de la Ciudad de Buenos Aires. *Informe de resultados del Proyecto Jurisdiccional de Evaluación de Nivel Medio 3° año (2010-2011)*. Buenos Aires: Ministerio de Educación, 2012. Print.

Myers, Greg. "The Pragmatics of Politeness in Scientific Articles." *Applied Linguistics*, 10.1 (1989): 1-35. Print.

Navarro, Federico. ¿Qué escribir en la escuela? Análisis de una propuesta institucional de escritura a través del currículum. *Bellaterra Journal of Teaching & Learning Language & Literature (Universitat Autònoma de Barcelona)* 6.1 (2013): 18-34. Web.

Navarro, Federico, and Andrea Revel Chion. *Escribir para aprender. Disciplinas y escritura en la escuela secundaria*. Buenos Aires: Paidós, 2013. Print.

Revel Chion, A. "Hablar y escribir ciencias." *Educar en ciencias*. Eds. Elsa Meinardi, Leonardo González Galli, Andrea Revel Chion, and María Victoria Plaza. Buenos Aires: Paidós, 2010. 163-90. Print.

Rivard, Leonard P., and Stanley B. Straw. "The Effect of Talk and Writing on Learning Science: An Exploratory Study." *Science Education* 84.5 (2000): 566-93. Web.

Rose, David, and J. R. Martin. *Learning to Write, Reading to Learn. Genre, Knowledge and Pedagogy in the Sydney School*. London: Equinox, 2012. Print.

CHAPTER 5

COLLABORATING ON WRITING-TO-LEARN IN NINTH-GRADE SCIENCE: WHAT IS COLLABORATION—AND HOW CAN WE SUSTAIN IT?

Danielle Myelle-Watson, Deb Spears, David Wellen, Michael McClellan, and Brad Peters

Other contributors to this volume note that in high school and university partnerships, teachers often want extended time to collaborate with professors so they can learn more about developing specific methods relevant to their own subject areas (Cox and Gimbel, Chapter 2). However, high school circumstances and practices can hinder the collaboration (Beaumont, Pydde, and Tschirpke, Chapter 7). Keeping communication lines open is critical.

In the project recounted here, three science teachers, a high school reading specialist, and a university coordinator of WAC collaborated for a year and a half in a project sponsored by an Illinois state grant from Promoting Achievement through Literacy Skills (PALS). Modeled on a previous study at the same high school, the science writing project provided teachers with university credit for a semester's course that the reading specialist and the WAC coordinator had co-taught on site many times before (Peters 64-66). The following year, the teachers implemented what they learned with continued support from the PALS grant and ongoing collaboration with the reading specialist and the WAC coordinator (McClellen et al.).

Similar to other chapters in this volume, the project matched materials and aims to the needs and interests of the teachers (McMullen-Light, Chapter 6). A chief concern among the teachers was how writing-to-learn might help ninth-grade students attain "scientific literacy," especially with the emphasis that the new Common Core Standards put on "Career and College Readiness Anchor Standards for Writing" in their science classes (States Standards Initiative 63-66; Cox and Gimbel). Historically, educators have identified science literacy as:

- A cultural force in the modern world
- Preparation for the workplace

- Applicable to everyday living
- A trait of informed citizenship
- A particular way of examining nature
- An approach to understanding scientific reports or discussions in popular media
- A means of appreciating the aesthetics of natural laws and phenomena
- A willingness to make use of scientific expertise
- A way to critique and use technology ethically. (DeBoer 591-93)

But in a 78.7% high-poverty urban district where the teachers' school was on academic watch, where standardized tests predominated, and where the majority of non-college bound students only needed to complete two courses in science to graduate, such goals seemed out of reach for many (Illinois Interactive Report Card; Rockford Public Schools 7). How could writing-to-learn help?

During the spring semester prior to implementing the project, the teachers studied resources on writing-to-learn. Then, they composed and experimented with sets of sequenced writing prompts that clarified scientific concepts embedded in class discussions, small-group interaction, and above all, laboratory work. They piloted and evaluated the prompts, using a rubric that other teachers in the same school had developed for an earlier project (Peters 65). In consultation with the high school reading specialist, the teachers decided that all of their next-year courses—two honors sections of biology, five "average" sections of biology, and seven sections of physical science—would engage in four National Writing Project practices:

- Plan informal writing at least twice a month
- Discuss writing strategies in the context of course content
- Do some form of redrafting
- Collect, examine, and reflect on the writing. (Nagin 44)

The following summer, the district serendipitously recruited the three teachers and their colleagues in other high schools to design four quarterly tests in biology and physical science as a move toward instruction-based assessment (Gallagher 58-59). District faculty closely aligned the tests with the curriculum. The three science teachers felt the quarterly tests could help them gauge the gains of writing-to-learn in comparison with their students' district peers.

When the new academic year began, the teachers agreed to form a "Professional Learning Community" (PLC) that would meet every two weeks. In the PLC meetings, they would review and revise prompts that addressed key concepts in the curriculum. They would discuss samples of student responses, analyze any problems or concerns that came up, and examine the quarterly test results. They would also provide written reflections on each quarter's progress.

The first quarter of the next year's collaboration showed great promise. Everyone attended the PLC meetings. The teachers regularly consulted with the reading specialist between the meetings. Both the biology and physical science students responded well to informal writing. In all achievement levels, students improved substantially in their lab reports and scored approximately ten percentage points higher than their district peers in the first-quarter district tests. Correlated test scores were also statistically significant.

However, the second quarter did not proceed in the same way. Unexpected issues interrupted the PLC meetings, forcing cancellations and sporadic attendance. Although the reading specialist tried to help them all keep up, lack of adequate collaboration as a group had a negative impact. Biology students did much less writing-to-learn than expected. Physical science students (approximately 30% of whom were special education students) struggled with prompts that intimidated or confused them.

After the second quarter, the nature of the collaboration changed. Debriefing among the teachers as a cohort waned. Maintaining a sustainable structure for communication became a challenge (similar to Beaumont, Pydde, and Tschirpke, Chapter 7). Because the project took place at the high school, the reading specialist and WAC coordinator could still meet with teachers individually. Nevertheless, prompts in biology were assigned unevenly through the third and fourth quarters. It was difficult to tell if writing-to-learn made a difference. Honors biology students received quarterly test scores that remained the same as, or dropped even lower than, their district peers. Yet average biology students achieved slightly higher test scores, and one third-semester biology class earned scores that were statistically significant.

On the other hand, after the teachers readjusted some of their practices, physical science students either kept on responding to two sets of prompts per quarter or focused more on writing well-developed conclusions to lab reports. These at-risk students accomplished statistically significant test scores in the third and fourth quarters.

In addition to correlating the quarterly test scores between students who wrote to learn and district students who did not, the teachers collected their students' "write-to-learn" folders to be read, ranked, and examined at the end of the academic year. Descriptive statistics suggested that the frequency and consistency of writing-to-learn tasks were important variables, in addition to the impact of changes in collaboration among the teachers, the reading specialist, and the WAC coordinator. Accordingly, the story that follows is as much a study of the dynamics of collaboration as it is a study of how writing-to-learn affects student learning outcomes.

WHY WRITE TO LEARN? A THEORETICAL BASIS FOR ENHANCING SCIENTIFIC LITERACY

National studies show how writing-to-learn can help students "learn more deeply" and attain "higher achievement in science" (Peery 17-18, 21; Reeves; Rivard). Moreover, a study conducted by the National Survey of Student Engagement and the National Council of Writing Program Administrators claims that in the most successful classroom experiences, "the amount of pages students wrote was less important for deep learning and gains than interactive writing, meaning-making, and clear expectations" (Anderson et al. 1). This claim is supported by the earlier findings of Johannessen, Kahn, and Walter who asserted that sequenced writing-to-learn prompts can yield "dramatic gains in only a short time," enabling high school students to make "essential thinking strategies ... part of their repertoire" when they encounter new material (5, 22). However, those sequenced prompts must be clustered around a specific concept and designed to break a complex thinking process into more manageable steps (Johannessen, Kahn, and Walter 5). Such claims impressed the science teachers particularly because the reading specialist had participated in a previous study of writing-to-learn in their high school, which implied that all students—even low achievers—could "produce statistically significant learning outcomes" (Peters 85).

The science teachers already asked students to write a fair amount. Lab guidelines sharpened the students' observational and procedural skills regularly. These questions from a physical science lab on magnets are typical:

- Place iron filings on a blank piece of white paper to create a magnetic field around a bar magnet. Draw the magnetic field lines.
- What observations do you make?
- Place two bar magnets so the north pole of one is close to the south pole of another. Draw the field lined near the poles.
- What observation can you make?

Furthermore, one teacher provided her students with the following guidelines on "How to write the different parts" of "Power Conclusions" to their lab reports:

- Reference to hypothesis—"I thought that ..." (if ... then statement)
- Reflection on hypothesis—"I found out ... therefore my hypothesis was ...."
- Reference to specific data—"My data showed that ..."
- Error analysis—"Doing _____ may have affected my results"; "I forgot to ..."; "I could have improved on my _____ skill(s) and this would have ..."

- Future research—"I would like to investigate more about _____ because ..."; "Knowing _____ will help me to ..."; "We should repeat the experiment because ..." (adapted from Pierce and Shellhaas)

Students also wrote papers requiring Internet research, e.g., reports on famous scientists' discoveries, or detailed profiles of simple to complex animal life.

All the same, the science teachers welcomed exercises that have succeeded in science classes nationwide—e.g., freewriting, RAFTs (role/audience/form/topic), the Science Writing Heuristic, Cornell notes, reading logs, interpretations of graphs, and even poetry—(Chabot and Tomkiewicz 53-55; Childers and Lowry 1; Hohenshell and Hand 271; Keys 116; Peery 127-51; Petersen 99). They recognized that different written practices could also help their students acquire and negotiate the disciplinary knowledge they needed to become scientifically literate (Navarro and Ravel Chion, Chapter 4). Most important, they were interested in composing sequenced prompts that scaffolded students' thinking strategies around a specific scientific concept (Johannessen, Kahn, and Walter 3-4; Wood, Bruner, and Ross 89-90).

During the onsite course, the teachers also questioned and re-examined their assumptions about how they taught scientific literacy in their classrooms. For example, one science teacher always asked his students to memorize an acronym similar to the Science Writing Heuristic: "P.H.E.O.I.C." (define a problem, form a hypothesis, experiment, observe, interpret data, and make a conclusion). He would occasionally quiz them or ask them to recite it. But after a lively discussion with his colleagues about how and why students so often failed to translate this acronym into well-written lab reports, he wondered if he was engaging his students in "knowledge telling" rather than "knowledge transforming" (Bereiter and Scardamalia, 1987; Rivard and Straw 586). He went on to compose the following set of sequenced prompts to help students apply the heuristic more *meaningfully* and *critically*:

- Define science, pseudoscience, hypothesis, and law.
- Identify steps of the scientific method for a classmate who was absent in class the day we reviewed it. Explain why you think scientists follow these steps.
- Describe all the parts of a controlled experiment. Give reasons why you think it's important to include a control group and an experimental group. Remember to discuss the effects of independent and dependent variables.
- Develop a well-thought out set of instructions that anyone could follow for the lab we did on potatoes. Include guides for analyzing the data and drawing a conclusion from a hypothesis and its test.

He assigned these prompts at intervals over a two-week period in one class and asked students to talk over their answers each time they wrote. He reported back to his colleagues that it allowed him to intersperse the writing with small-group lab work and what McCann et al. call "authentic discussion": engaging the students directly in critical thinking about the concept he was teaching, rather than requiring them merely to recite it (2-3). In sum, he and his colleagues deduced that writing-to-learn could become part of several "language-based activities" that contributed to the complex changes that enabled their students to acquire scientific literacy (Rivard 438).

This high-caliber collaboration occurred among the science teachers throughout the semester's preparatory course, giving rise to a "WACommunity" that reflected "a true culture of writing" (Cox and Gimbel, Chapter 2; McMullen-Light, Chapter 6). In turn, the reading specialist and the WAC coordinator gained rich insights about the value of teachers applying their disciplinary knowledge to assignment design to address students' specific learning problems.

INSTRUCTION-BASED ASSESSMENT: A RESPONSE TO STANDARDIZED TESTS

The district's summer decision to ask all science teachers to develop quarterly tests came at a good time. Some state boards of education are discovering what teachers and scholars have known for years. Too much emphasis on standardized tests not only "squelches teaching and learning creativity"—it also "eliminates the need for critical thought" (College Readiness Project, Phase II; Hillocks 136). Yet a recent national survey shows that secondary teachers care a lot about the accountability that tests produce, as long as it does not force them to neglect important aspects of their curriculum (Sunderman, Kim, and Orfield 124). Teachers in a few states have found instruction-driven assessment based on locally designed tests especially compelling, because it enables them to parse assessments throughout the year, increasing the possibility of using test scores to discover and redress their students' needs before those students leave the classroom or fail (Gallagher 63). Instruction-driven assessment can even encourage teachers to develop individual education plans for students, using writing-to-learn, portfolios and "student-friendly rubrics to help students understand learning expectations" (Gallagher 67). Science scholars in Washington suggest such an approach may in fact reveal that "*how* students learn could be more important than *what* they learn" (College Readiness Project, Phase II).

Nonetheless, it was unusual for the school district to initiate the quarterly tests. As with other large urban districts, teachers often felt "alienated from core decisions about [...] instruction," where "district objectives, large criterion-referenced tests, and textbooks" dictated the curriculum (Gallagher 65). Some faculty suspected the district intended the tests to enforce cookie-cutter syllabi throughout its four high schools. But after years of reserving nearly a month to prepare students for the Prairie State Achievement Examination (PSAE) and the ACT, the three science teachers cautiously welcomed tests that mirrored what they actually taught. They saw how the quarterly tests could help "develop and refine their curriculum, instruction, professional development ... and assessment," above all because the tests were also aligned with "power standards" adapted from the Illinois learning standards for science (Gallagher 64-65; Illinois State Board of Education). Moreover, as in other districts that have tried instruction-driven assessment, the quarterly tests would let the science teachers give "heightened attention to particular groups of students, including low-income students, English language learners [ELL], and ethnic or racial groups" (Gallagher 65). The quarterly tests bolstered the collaboration accordingly as they began in the preparatory course. The reading specialist and the WAC coordinator were excited that this approach to assessment could take the collaboration to an even higher level, making the project relevant to the whole district.

While these teacher-designed assessments clearly established expectations for content coverage at a certain pace, the three science teachers still noted places where they could apply writing-to-learn most advantageously. The tests also left room in the curriculum for the teachers to address important issues that required expanding upon and connecting. For instance, could the physical science curriculum include a short review of earth science—a subject covered only in middle school—even though 25% of the PSAE questions focused on it? They wanted to try.

After studying the tests in a PLC meeting, the teachers decided the physical science prompts should address the topics of:

- The relationship between matter and energy
- Elements, compounds, and mixtures
- The earth and its atmosphere
- Atomic structure
- Chemical reactions (combustion of gas)
- The scientific problem-solving process
- Common uses of electricity
- Electrical circuits
- Magnetic fields and uses of magnets

Meanwhile, the teachers decided the biology prompts should address the topics of:

- Characteristics of living things
- Biotic and abiotic factors in ecosystems
- Plant and animal cells
- Differentiating mitosis and meiosis
- Cell specialization and embryonic development
- DNA replication
- Inheritance of genetic traits
- Evolution of genetic traits

Because one teacher taught both physical science and biology, it seemed optimal for all three to work together and share the prompts they were creating anew, rather than each teacher create a separate set of prompts. The alignment that the teachers sought between writing-to-learn and the quarterly tests went beyond mere attempts to teach to the tests. They hoped to begin recovering what a decade of No Child Left Behind had done in their district to narrow the curriculum, to emphasize lower-level skills, and to decrease teacher and student engagement in the development of science literacy (Gallagher 39).

Although the three teachers, the reading specialist, and the WAC coordinator collaborated closely upon the prompts for the first quarter—discussing and revising them in the PLC meetings, as well as examining samples of student's corresponding work—the rest of the year's prompts on the topic lists remained unfinished. As chance would have it, the teachers' plan to continue collaborating on the prompts did not account for the unexpected.

THE UNEXPECTED: FIRST-QUARTER PACING FOR DIFFERENT LEVELS OF ACHIEVERS

Pacing was one of the biggest problems the science teachers encountered during the first quarter of their implementation of writing-to-learn. Although the instruction-based, quarterly tests focused on the actual curriculum that teachers taught, and the Common Core Standards encouraged richer, more "varied genres and purposes of writing," the district hadn't abandoned the PSAE or ACT, which still emphasized shallow coverage over deep learning—pressuring the teachers to move through the curriculum "more quickly than they would if their professional judgment were their guide" (Cox and Gimbel, Chapter 2; Gallagher 65-66). Such conflicting exigencies could only complicate the science teachers' attempts to extend instruction "by doing more exploratory learning and more constructivist learning" through scaffolding (Gallagher 66).

To illustrate, one teacher—Dawn—had her students write "bell ringers" at the beginning of classes, to provide them with the "multiple writing tasks across connected topics" that she had learned to design (Hand, Hohenshell, and Prain 344). She would spend a few minutes getting the students to focus on responding to the bell ringers, and then she would lead a discussion of the students' responses. Next, she would go on to address the day's lesson, which connected directly to the bell ringer. After several days and two to three bell ringers, she would give the students the longer prompt to address. She found out, however, that the impact of the bell ringers differed between her average and her honors students in biology. When she did a series of lessons on biotic and abiotic factors, one lesson began with the bell ringer: "Explain the difference between a rock and a wooden board." Then, she introduced the terms and spent time discussing the distinctions. The next lesson began with: "Define biotic and abiotic. Write about three different objects in this classroom that are biotic and three that are abiotic." She then provided the students with several scenarios that would affect biotic and abiotic factors—e.g., a hurricane, an oil spill, over-grazing, building a golf course, a nuclear leak, highway construction. She broke the students into groups, each group to analyze how one scenario would affect biotic and abiotic factors. They then presented their group analyses. The following day, she assigned the longer prompt:

> Analyze one of the scenarios we discussed. Identify several biotic and abiotic factors, and explain how each of these factors would be affected by the scenario. Then hypothesize if/how these biological situations could return to their natural or normal state over time.

Dawn used this sequence with both her honors-level and average classes, just as she had with a previous sequence of prompts on the characteristics of living things. She found out the honors students had "the cognitive tools and the conceptual building blocks necessary" for completing the task (Rivard and Straw 587), but the average students did not. She needed to supplement the task with more follow-up prompts and class discussion before they, too, could distinguish between biotic/abiotic and apply their knowledge to real-life scenarios. She did so, but barely covered the material her students needed for the first-quarter test.

The experience with her biology students made Dawn sensitive to her physical science classes as well. Many of her ELL and special education students not only needed more scaffolding, but also always needed more time to complete the culminating prompts (Lee et al. 33; Stretch and Osborn 4). When she gave these students this extra help and time, they performed nearly on par with their higher-achieving peers—though their work showed less detail and grammatical fluency. This finding suggested that even her low-achieving students could benefit from writing-to learn, contrary to opposite claims (Bangert-Drowns, Hurley, and Wilkinson 6, 53).

So a dilemma surfaced. Could Dawn ignore that her lower-achieving students would learn almost as well as her higher-achieving students if she simply slowed down the pace of the curriculum? Her physical science students performed quite well on the material they had covered for the first-quarter test, but when the results of their writing-to-learn compelled her to take longer to accommodate their learning pace, she knew they would fail on the material they had not covered. Unlike Mike, her colleague who taught physical science exclusively, she had no special education teacher assigned to her class to help her physical science students keep up.

Dawn cut back considerably on write-to-learn prompts and focused on helping students improve conclusions to their lab reports instead. The students did three to four lab reports per quarter. This way, she could manage the curricular pace. She reasoned that the guidelines she used for writing the conclusions would provide similar scaffolding. The WAC coordinator noted her reasoning was supported by researchers who state: "scientific writing genres should be explicitly taught, so that all children might have access to the discursive power of scientific texts" (Halliday and Martin xi, 2-4; Keys 118). Above all, researchers assert how young learners affected by poverty and categorized as "low achievers" are especially disadvantaged when not taught explicitly to write scientific texts (Keys 118-19; Rivard 424-25).

David, a teacher who taught only biology classes for the year, developed another way to pace writing-to-learn in the first quarter. Influenced by the Common Core Standards' emphasis on students reading and integrating facts, definitions, and details from informative texts into their written work, he introduced short articles to supplement the biology textbook and labs (States Standards Initiatives 65). For example, students could read an article and formulate simple experiments that tested the claims they read. One article asserted that fish could see and were attracted to different kinds of colors. The students experimented with goldfish and multicolored glow sticks to verify the article's claim. Then they wrote lab reports that involved "peer review, collaborative problem solving, [and] student partner revision teams" (Mullin and Childers 26; Zimmet 106). David also had the students read the articles, write brief summaries, discuss them, and then revise what they had learned (DeBoer 592-93). After reading an article on scientists who planted a "smart gene" into mice DNA, one student wrote in her summary that this was a stupid idea. Why did the world need smarter mice? However, when her class discussed the article, learned its vocabulary, grasped why the experiment was conducted, and questioned the ethical implications, she rewrote her summary, saying that she now saw what the article was all about. She still thought that biologically engineering smarter mice made no practical sense, but if it led to making humans smarter, would it help her learn better and perform well on tests? Would it give some people an advantage over others? Yet again, what if gene-planting affected human brains badly? Some of David's most successful classes were centered on "sociopolitical and moral contexts" such as these that helped develop his students' science literacy (Soliday 67).

Although pleased that his students performed well on the first-quarter exam, David also fell behind in the curriculum. He decided to include only one write-to-learn task in the second quarter. He eliminated the shorter prompts that led up to it, using them instead to guide class discussion. In the third and fourth quarters, he did the same, to see if relying more heavily upon "collaborative talk as a heuristic" might compensate for cut-backs in writing (Rivard 424).

Mike, who taught physical science courses exclusively, was the only one who stayed with the plan to do two sets of prompts each quarter. He made sure that students responded in writing to the shorter, scaffolding prompts, interspersing their written responses with class discussion. For instance, he would have students compose a T-chart to help them organize and define new terms, then he would conduct a discussion of those terms in the context of the scientific concept he was introducing. Next, he would have the students do a lab that applied those concepts. At that point, students could illustrate or graph their findings as well, as Childers and Lowry recommend (n. pag.). Once the labs provided students with the knowledge base they needed, Mike had them write comparisons of their data (Rivard and Straw 586).

Yet this pattern pressed Mike for time in the second quarter as well, so he combined the shorter scaffolding prompts with the longer prompt into a kind of step-by-step, essayistic quiz. When he initiated these essayistic quizzes, the results were disappointing. He did not provide enough class discussion or build in enough shorter prompts to support the students written explanations of atomic structure or combustion in a gas engine. So he designed later quizzes as part of a "recursive cycle" with "students applying or practicing each small step" that he modeled, while he or his aide checked that "the class as a whole [was] succeeding on each successive step" (Schmoker n. pag.). Moreover, he carefully strategized the best time to schedule the write-to-learn exercises in relation to lab work. This approach got much better results. Conversely, Mike discovered that if students did lab work, recorded observations, and studied results on one day, but wrote the conclusions to lab reports on the following day, they processed what they had learned and composed better conclusions (McClellan n. pag.).

Ironically, what each science teacher found out about their students' learning needs caused the tightly knit collaboration to unravel. Deb, the reading specialist, and Brad, the WAC coordinator, realized that they could not rally the teachers back to the original collaborative model without challenging each teacher's decision to incorporate write-to-learn principles in her or his own way. While the group recovered a schedule of meeting regularly, the collaboration with the teachers occurred on a much more individual basis—often with only one teacher attending at a time. Although Dawn and David composed a few more prompts together for their biology students, they stayed mostly with what they felt more comfortable doing, according to their first-quarter adaptations. And as Mike focused independently on implementing the physical science prompts he wrote, Dawn focused on guiding her biology and physical science students alike to write "power conclusions." For good and thoughtful reasons, the teachers might have lost track altogether of what each was doing had Deb and Brad not continued to compare and analyze with each the successes or problems that the others encountered as the year progressed. This adapted model of collaboration sacrificed a uniform approach for an individuated approach. It not only enriched the project's outcomes, but it also complicated and altered the disciplinary conversation that the PLC had sustained to that point.

Unfortunately, other issues compounded the teachers' efforts to keep pace with the curriculum. Student absences and truancy were always high. Each of the teachers walked into classes on days when 50% or even more of the students were missing. Student mobility presented another challenge. Dawn recounted one week in the second quarter when ten new students showed up in a section of physical science. Combining drop-outs with new arrivals, each teacher's roster for each class included a minimum of five to seven students who would not finish out the year, and the same number of students who might be added at any time.

The probability of a strike during the second quarter complicated the situation further. The teachers had to cancel three PLC sessions to attend union meetings instead. A conservative Board of Education had threatened to raise teachers' insurance to $800 per month, cut 138 jobs, increase class sizes from 26 students to 34 students, shut down four schools, eliminate five major programs, and cancel orders for new textbooks. Only the spring before, the district had closed or consolidated ten schools, slashed special education classes, and dropped 281 jobs (Bayer).[1]

Given these issues, the end-of-year results yielded a number of encouraging surprises.

THE IMPACT OF WRITING-TO-LEARN UPON INSTRUCTION-BASED ASSESSMENT

Although this project went in three different directions after the first quarter—reverting to the kinds of "fragmented individualism" that can characterize secondary teachers even when they belong to the same department—the quarterly tests provided an anchor that helped the teachers measure the effects of their varied approaches the rest of the year (Siskin 28-29).

During the first quarter, when all three science teachers incorporated two sets of write-to-learn prompts, the students' higher scores in David's and Dawn's combined biology classes differed from the other district classes by 11.72 percentage points (Table 1, below).[2]

Table 1: First-quarter biology

1ˢᵗ Quarter Biology Tests	№ of Questions	№ of Students	Possible Points	Avg. Points	Avg. % Correct
Biology students who did writing-to-learn	35	181	35	21.77	62.20%
District biology students	35	1369	35	17.67	50.48%

Biology students who wrote to learn outperformed the rest of the district on 89% of the questions. When a two-sample t-test compared the 181 writing-to-learn students with the 1369 ninth-grade district biology students, results yielded $t(68) = 2.94$, $p < .05$—suggesting less than a 5% probability that higher scores among writing-to-learn students were coincidental. The *effect size r* was also calculated with a result of .3—a medium effect—indicating that writing-to-learn had made a positive impact on the students' retention of biological concepts (Steinberg 366).

Scores in Mike's physical science classes were even more compelling (Table 2).[3]

Table 2: First-quarter physical science

1ˢᵗ Quarter Physical Science Tests	№ of Questions	№ of Students	Possible Points	Avg. Points	Avg. % Correct
Physical science students who did writing-to-learn	30	129	30	18.6	61.99%
District physical science Students	30	598	30	14.3	47.56%

Mike's 129 students who did writing-to-learn scored higher on 90% of the questions. The t-test showed that $t(58) = 3.06 < p\ .005$. There was less than a

.05% probability that coincidence could explain the percentage of correct answers among students in his classes, bolstered by a .4 *effect size r*—or large effect size.

Dawn's shift from prompts to a writing-to-learn (WTL) emphasis on better conclusions in lab reports had a moderate, upward effect on her average biology students' scores (Table 3), but the honors biology students' scores fluctuated in comparison to the rest of the district.

Table 3: Comparison of 2nd to 4th-quarter biology, write-to-learn emphasis on lab report conclusions/no known WTL emphasis

Achievement Levels, Biology	WTL Emphasis on Lab Report Conclusions	District—No Known WTL Emphasis
Average-2nd Quarter	47.88%	44.36%
Honors-2nd Quarter	59.05%	61.72%
Average-3rd Quarter	51.05%	42.88%
Honors-3rd Quarter	65.14%	63.86%
Average-4th Quarter	54.50%	51.26%
Honors-4th Quarter	65.10%	69.06%

Because the third-quarter percentage of correct answers for Dawn's 23 average students were so much higher, a t-test was run. Calculations showed that $t(60) = 2.07 < p\ .25$, with a .256 or medium *effect size r*. These results suggested that a WTL emphasis on lab report conclusions might account for her average biology students' higher percent of correct answers, at least in the third-quarter test, if not on the second and fourth quarters as well (Table 4). The less positive impact that a WTL emphasis on lab report conclusions had upon honors students will be addressed in the discussion section.

Table 4: Third-quarter biology, Dawn's "average class"

3rd Quarter Biology, Dawn's Average Class	№ of Questions	№ of Students	Possible Points	Avg. Points	Avg. % Correct
Students with WTL Emphasis on Lab Report Conclusions	31	23	31	15.83	51.05%
District biology students	31	744	31	13.29	42.88%

The most pronounced correct-answer percentages between WTL classes and the rest of the district came from physical science during the third and fourth quarters. It was apparent that both writing-to-learn prompts and a WTL emphasis on lab report conclusions pushed all of the classes' percent of correct answers above the students' district peers (Tables 5 and 6).

Table 5: Third-quarter physical science

3rd Quarter Physical Science Tests	№ of Questions	№ of Students	Possible Points	Avg. Points	Avg. % Correct
Physical science students who did writing-to-learn	30	119	30	19.2	63.84%
District physical science students	30	494	30	14.3	47.61%

The 119 third-quarter physical science students who wrote to learn scored 63.84% more correct answers than the 494 students in the rest of the district, yielding a t-test of $t(58) = 4.75$, $p < .005$—less than a .05% possibility that the impact of writing-to-learn was coincidental. *Effect size r* was large at .53. Given the high percentage of ELL and special education students, these results were worth noting.

In the fourth quarter, the 111 physical science students who wrote to learn scored an average of 65.33% correct answers, while the 448 district students who did not write to learn scored 44.08%.

Table 6: Fourth-quarter physical science

4th Quarter Physical Science Tests	№ of Questions	№ of Students	Possible Points	Avg. Points	Avg. % Correct
Physical science students who did writing-to-learn	30	111	30	19.59	65.33%
District physical science students	30	448	30	13.44	44.08%

The t-test revealed that $t(58) = 6.79$, $p < .005$, or less than a .05% coincidence that writing-to-learn had no impact. *Effect size r* came in at .66, which was large.

The least encouraging results derived from David's increased emphasis on class discussion to compensate for less writing-to-learn. Table 7 shows a possible negative impact—especially for average biology students in the third quarter.

Table 7: Effects of increased class discussion and decreased writing-to-learn

Achievement Levels, Biology	Increased Discussion, Decreased WTL	District—No Known WTL Emphasis
Average-2nd Quarter	45.16%	44.36%
Honors-2nd Quarter	60.69%	61.72%
Average-3rd Quarter	37.41%	43.84%
Honors-3rd Quarter	62.01%	63.86%
Average-4th Quarter	50.29%	51.26%
Honors-4th Quarter	49.13%	51.26%

At the end of the year, student folders were also collected to get a sense of what quality of work had been achieved, and how the work might provide insights about differences among honors, average, and lower-achieving students. For students' responses to the write-to-learn prompts, the science teachers used the rubric in Table 8 to gauge their students' comprehension of task, content, thinking strategies, and language use (Johannessen, Kahn, and Walter 11-12; Peters 65-66).

The WAC coordinator then selected student folders that contained at least 60% of the assigned prompts, rated them, and calculated the averages of the two ratings per folder.

A rating of 8 out of 12 possible points meant that student folders had met expectations. Seventy-four percent of 50 honors biology students who turned in folders completed a minimum 60% of all writing-to-learn prompts assigned. The overall average rating for those honors biology folders was 9.56, with a S.D. of 1.5. Fifty percent of 109 "average" biology students who turned in folders completed a minimum 60% of all writing-to-learn prompts. The overall average rating for the "average biology" folders was 8.35 with a S.D. of 1.1. Forty-six percent of the 163 physical science students who turned in folders completed 60% of all writing-to learn prompts. The overall average rating for the physical science folders was 8.05 with a S.D. of 1.2. Fifty-four percent of honors biology students achieved a rating of 10 or higher, while 9% of the average biology students, and 4% of the physical science students, rated in the same range. Two percent of honors biology students, 6% of average biology students, and 9% of physical science students rated 7 or lower.

Table 8: Rubric

CRITERIA	Exceeds expectations 3	Meets expectations 2	Misses expectations 1
Comprehension of Task—your ability to respond informally to what the writing prompt asks	You understand and follow instructions exactly. ☐	You understand and follow instructions adequately ☐	You misunderstand or disregard instructions. ☐
Content—your ability to convey knowledge of course content received from reading or listening	You provide very accurate information and thorough detail ☐	You provide accurate information and sufficient detail. ☐	You provide inaccurate information and/ or insufficient detail. ☐
Strategies—your ability to apply, analyze, back up, compare, classify, critique, define, describe, evaluate, explain, exemplify, graph, hypothesize, illustrate, interpret, observe, organize, predict, question, reflect, review, show cause-effect, solve, summarize, or synthesize.	You show clear control over the strategy or strategies that the prompt requires. ☐	You show satisfactory evidence of understanding and practicing required strategies. ☐	You show little or no evidence of understanding required strategies. ☐
Language use—your ability to write a readable response and use conventions of grammar and punctuation	Your response is articulate; errors minimal. ☐	Your response is easy to read; errors don't prevent understanding. ☐	Your response is hard to read/ understand; errors confuse. ☐

IN RETROSPECT

In terms of student learning outcomes, perhaps the most thought-provoking finding in the foregoing data has to do with the performance of students who were categorized as low achievers. After a year of consistent writing-to-learn, they successfully demonstrated what they retained in the quarterly tests. Rivard points out: "The ways in which learning strategies have traditionally been utilized in the classroom have effectively denied equal access to knowledge for all students" (424). Yet as he points out, the research literature—including this project—

> suggests that classroom activities which emphasize conceptual understanding, real-life applications, language use, and small-group work may be particularly effective for enhancing the learning of students who have traditionally been marginalized by the educational system: low-ability students, underachievers, and potential school leavers. (Rivard 424)

Moreover, the data in this study indicate that so-called low achievers are capable of responding well to specific instruction in specialized forms of disciplinary writing when it is structured "to foster more reflective thinking and enhanced student learning from laboratory activities" (Bazerman et al. 42). The same apparently held true to a lesser extent for "average" biology students who more sporadically wrote to learn.

The drop in honors students' test scores when they decreased writing-to-learn coincides with other research that shows "high achievers may benefit more from the use of writing" than average or low achievers—for them, especially, "the use of writing enhances learning more than just talk" (Rivard 432). This project suggests that writing-to-learn has a far more substantial effect upon high achievers than previously thought, and they achieved less when they stopped doing it. Furthermore, the results seem to reiterate the National Writing Project's recommendation of planning write-to-learn activities a minimum of twice a month (Nagin 44).

Nonetheless, as all three science teachers noticed, if combined consistently with writing-to-learn, "opportunities for all students to engage in extended dialogues signals the expectation that all learners will meet challenging academic standards" (McCann, Johannessen, Kahn, and Flanagan 6-7; Rivard and Straw 567-68). The progressively higher physical science test scores indicated as much.

Commercially prepared tests that do not align with the local curriculum may not measure such success. Indeed, such tests may have held sway over the potential of low and average-achieving students for far too long. Local, instruction-driven assessment offers real promise for counteracting their detrimental effects, above all if this assessment is aligned with state standards and the national Common Core Standards. As the data here shows, if teachers can be encouraged to find the best, most workable methods for themselves to pace their students through the curriculum, they may use instruction-driven assessment combined with informal writing activities "in a strategic way throughout the school year ... to the extent that students [don't] even know when they [are] being formally assessed and when they [are] simply carrying out 'regular' classroom activities" (Gallagher 63-64).

In terms of collaboration, this project's findings are equally thought-provoking. While some contributors to this volume rightly assert that even short-term partnerships between high schools and colleges or universities can have a positive impact, productive collaboration often must begin with some kind of formalized arrangement on the part of the post-secondary institution (Cox and Gimbel, Chapter 2; McMullen-Light, Chapter 6; Smith, Chapter 9). High school faculty not only need opportunities to learn, but also need to apply principles of writing across the curriculum and discuss the results. It helps tremendously if a project includes a high school faculty member who can co-facilitate, and at the same time relate with or convey the teachers' circumstances and concerns (Peters 63). Conducting several projects at the same school increases the likelihood of success, as one project informs another (McClellan n. pag.). Grants or other sources of funding provide participants with the incentive to keep the project going (McClellan n. pag.; Peters 63;). As McMullen claims, "In all aspects of WAC, context is everything," so if professors can collaborate on site with teachers, it helps tremendously (Chapter 6). Establishing "joint commitments" to a sustained time to meet and regularly work together must be set up for exchanging ideas and keeping goals equally in perspective (Blumner and Childers 94). Mapping out a plan and setting specific milestones, even if they only serve as a point of departure, enable participants to stay focused.

In addition, participants of such projects—in large American public schools, at least—should probably realize that the current culture of testing and standards mitigates against a "culture of collaboration," especially when those standards are imposed rather than adapted through collective activity (Siskin 28). For example, "Logistical constraints of size, time, and space" complicate the situation, engaging teachers in a kind of "parallel piecework" in their departments, where they are more likely to "work alone, learn alone, and [...] derive their most important personal satisfactions alone" (Huberman 22-23; Siskin 29). Even when collective activity occurs and collaboration is successfully sustained, the pull in the opposite direction is strong. Participants will want to find a system by which they can analyze and reconfigure their collaborative model so that the project survives (Beaumont, Pydde, and Tschirpke, Chapter 7).

Ultimately, some outcomes might not be met. Some problems will not be resolved. But recognizing this much allows for new discoveries and insights to emerge, as well as guidance for another project, another time.

NOTES

1. In fact, a three-day strike did take place later in the school year.

2. In an earlier publication on this study (McClellan et al. 2012) errata occurred because of a mistake in the formula that adjusted percentages of correct answers between the writing-to-learn classes and the rest of the district's classes. The errata are corrected here.

3. Dawn's Physical Science scores were removed from the data set because her students hadn't been able to cover all the material on the 1st quarter test.

WORKS CITED

Anderson, Paul, Chris Anson, Bob Gonyea, and Chuck Paine. "Summary: The Consortium for the Study of Writing in College." Handout. Council of Writing Program Administrators Summer Conference, Minneapolis, MN. Web. 17 July 2009. <http://nsse.indiana.edu/webinars/TuesdaysWithNSSE/2009_09_22_UsingResultsCSWC/Webinar Handout from WPA 2009.pdf>.

Bangert-Drowns, Robert, Marlene Hurley, and Barbara Wilkinson. "The Effects of School-Based Writing-to-Learn Interventions on Academic Achievement: A Meta-Analysis." *Review of Educational Research* 74.1 (Spring 2004): 29-58. Print.

Bayer, Cathy (2011, March 3). "Administration's Proposed Cuts." *Rockford Register Star.* Web. 3 Nov. 2011. <http://www.rrstar.com/carousel/x1174964897/Rockford-School-Board-still-has-3-1-million-more-in-cuts-to-make>.

Bazerman, Charles, Joseph Little, Lisa Bethel, Teri Chavkin, Danielle Fouquette, and Janet Garufis. *Reference Guide to Writing Across the Curriculum.* West Lafayette, IN: Parlor Press. Fort Collins: WAC Clearinghouse, 2005. Print.

Bereiter, Carl, and Marlene Scardamalia. *The Psychology of Written Composition.* Hillsdale: Erlbaum, 1987. Print.

Blumner, Jacob, and Pamela Childers. "Building Better Bridges: What Makes High School-College WAC Collaborations Work?" *The WAC Journal* 22 (2011): 91-101. Web. 11 November 2011.

Chabot, Chris, and Warren Tomkiewicz. "Writing in the Natural Science Department." *Writing Across the Curriculum* 9 (1998): 52-59. Web. 17 November 2014.

Childers, Pamela and Michael Lowry. "Connecting Visuals to Written Text and Written Text to Visuals in Science." *Across the Disciplines* 3 (2005): n. pag. Web. 7 Feb. 2011. <http://wac.colostate.edu/atd/visual/childers_lowry.cfm>.

College Readiness Project, An Initiative of the Higher Education Coordinating

Board to Define English and Science College Readiness in Washington State. Phase II (2008-09) Science Teams. Web. 17 June 2013. <https://web.archive.org/web/20130831194446/http:/collegereadinesswa.org/index.asp>

DeBoer, George. "Scientific Literacy: Another Look at Its Historical and Contemporary Meanings and Its Relationship to Science Education Reform." *Journal of Research in Science Teaching* 37.6 (2000): 582-601. Print.

Gallagher, Chris. *Reclaiming Assessment: A Better Alternative to the Accountability Agenda.* Portsmouth: Heinnemann, 2007. Print.

Halliday, Michael A. K., and James Martin. *Writing Science: Literacy and Discursive Power.* Pittsburgh: U of Pittsburgh P, 1993. Print.

Hand, Brian, Lisa Hohenshell, and Vaughan Prain. "Examining the Effect of Multiple Writing Tasks on Year 10 Biology Students' Understandings of Cell and Molecular Biology Concepts." *Instructional Science* 35.4 (2007): 343-73. Print.

Hohenshell, Liesl and Brian Hand. "Writing-to-Learn Strategies in Secondary School Cell Biology: A Mixed Method Study." *International Journal of Science Education* 28.2-3 (2006): 261-89. Print.

Hillocks, George, Jr. *The Testing Trap: How State Assessments Control Learning.* New York: Teachers College P, 2002. Print.

Huberman, Michael. "The Model of the Independent Artisan in Teachers' Professional Relations." *Teachers' Work: Individuals, Colleagues, and Contexts.* Ed. Judith Little and Milbrey McLaughlin. New York: Teachers College P, 1993. 11-50. Print.

Illinois Interactive Report Card. 2012. Web. 13 June 2013. <http://illinoisreportcard.com/School.aspx?schoolId=041012050250004>.

Illinois State Board of Education (ISBE). "Illinois Learning Standards: Science." Web. 14 March 2013. <http://www.isbe.state.il.us/ils/science/standards.htm>.

Johannessen, Larry R., Elizabeth Kahn, and Carolyn Walter. *Designing and Sequencing Prewriting Activities.* Urbana: National Council of Teachers of English, 1982. Print.

Keys, Carolyn. "Revitalizing Instruction in Scientific Genres: Connecting Knowledge Production with Writing-to-Learn in Science." *Science Education* 8.2 (1999): 115-30. Print.

Lee, Okhee, Jaime Maerten-Rivera, Randall Penfield, Kathryn LeRoy, and Walter Secada. "Science Achievement of English Language Learners in Urban Elementary Schools: Results of a First-Year Professional Development Intervention." *Journal of Research in Science Teaching* 45 (2008): 31-52. Print.

McCann, Thomas M., Larry Johannessen, Elizabeth Kahn, and Joseph Flanagan. *Talking in Class: Using Discussion to Enhance Teaching and Learning.* Urbana: National Council of Teachers of English, 2006. Print.

McClellan, Michael, Dawn Myelle-Watson, Brad Peters, Debora Spears, and David Wellen. "Writing Science in Hard Times." *Across the Disciplines,* 9.3 (2012). Web. 29 May 2013. <http://wac.colostate.edu/atd/second_educ/mcclellanetal.cfm>.

Mullin, Joan A. and Pamela B. Childers. "The Natural Connection: The WAC Program and the High School Writing Center." *The Clearing House: A Journal of Educational Strategies, Issues and Ideas,* 69.1 (1995): 24-26. Print.

Nagin, Carl. *Because Writing Matters: Improving Student Writing in Our Schools.* San Francisco: Jossey-Bass, 2003. Print.

Peery, Angela. *Writing Matters in Every Classroom.* Englewood: Lead+Learn P, 2009. Print.

Peters, Bradley. "Lessons about Writing to Learn from a University-High School Partnership." *Writing Program Administration: Journal of the Council of Writing Program Administrators* 34.2 (Spring 2011): 59-88. Print.

Petersen, Meg. "The Atomic Weight of Metaphor: Writing Poetry Across the Curriculum." *Writing Across the Curriculum* 12 (2001): 97-100. Print.

Pierce, Bettina, and David Shellhaas. "How to Write a 'Power Conclusion.'" Irvine Unified School District. Web. 3 June 2013.

Reeves, Douglas. *Accountability in Action: A Blueprint for Learning Organizations.* Englewood: Lead and Learn P, 2000. Print.

Rivard, Leonard P. "Are Language-Based Activities in Science Effective for All Students, Including Low Achievers?" *Science Education* 88 (2004): 420-42. Print.

Rivard, Leonard P., and Stanley Straw. "The Effect of Talk and Writing on Learning Science: An Exploratory Study." *Science Education* 84 (2000): 566-93. Print.

Rockford Public Schools. *High School Planning Guide 2011-2012.* Web. 5 Apr. 2013. <http://www3.rps205.com/District/Documents/Old%20Planning%20Guides/2011-2012_HSPlanningGuide.pdf>.

Schmoker, Mike. "The Lost Art of Teaching Soundly Structured Lessons." *Education Week,* 4 June 2013. Web. 10 June 2013. <http://www.edweek.org/tm/articles/2013/06/04/ fp_schmoker_lessons.html?tkn=QOTFkyJRaX-74kUeRDdmIZji7rSRatnFx%2B8n7&cmp=ENL-TU-NEWS1>.

Siskin, Leslie. "Subject Divisions." *The Subjects in Question: Departmental Organization and the High School.* Eds. Leslie Siskin and Judith Little. New York: Teachers College P, 1995. 23-47. Print.

Soliday, Mary. "Mapping Classroom Genres in a Science in Society Course." *Genre Across the Curriculum.* Eds. Anne Herrington and Charles Moran. Logan: Utah State UP, 2005. 65-82. Print.

States Standards Initiative. *Common Core Standards for English Language Arts and Literacy in History/ Social Studies, Science, and Technical Subjects.* Web. 5 Feb. 2012. <http://www.corestandards.org/ELA-Literacy>.

Steinberg, Wendy. *Statistics Alive!* Los Angeles: Sage Publications, 2008. Print.

Stretch, LoriAnn S., and Jason Osborn. "Extended Time Test Accommodation: Directions for Future Research and Practice." *Practical Assessment, Research, and Evaluation* 10 (2005): 1-8. Print.

Sunderman, Gail, James Kim, and Gary Orfield. *NCLB Meets School Realities: Lessons from the Field.* Thousand Oaks: Corwin P, 2005. Print.

Wood, David, Jerome Bruner, and Gail Ross. "The Role of Tutoring in Problem Solving." *Journal of Child Psychology and Psychiatry* 17 (1976): 89-100. Print.

Zimmet, Nancy. "Engaging the Disaffected: Collaborative Writing Across the Curriculum Projects." *English Journal* 90 (2000): 102-06. Print.

CHAPTER 6

IN OUR OWN BACKYARD: WHAT MAKES A COMMUNITY COLLEGE-SECONDARY SCHOOL CONNECTION WORK?

Mary McMullen-Light

In June of 2011, the Writing Across the Curriculum (WAC) Program at Metropolitan Community College-Longview provided a unique professional development experience for two-year college WAC coordinators, The WAC Institute for Community Colleges. The institute offered a hands-on, highly practical approach to designing and sustaining a WAC program within a two-year college setting. Bolstered by the success of the WAC Institute, Longview's WAC Program agreed to take on a very different kind of challenge the following year. At their request, create a meaningful WAC professional development experience for middle and high school teachers from a local Christian school (K-12). Responding to this request led to a relationship between the two schools, which yielded mutual pedagogical and intellectual benefits.

This chapter describes core elements of this pilot in partnering: sharing resources, helping establish a sustainable high school writing center, and providing meaningful WAC professional development opportunities for middle school and high school teachers, as well as the college instructors who helped facilitate the WAC workshop sessions.

The best way to establish such a relationship is to ground it with the premise that both groups enter the partnership with the belief that they have much to learn from each other. For example, significant time on the front end of this engagement involved putting people at ease, given that these academic environments are constructed very differently and have radically different missions: a private K-12 institution serving a very specific population of children and teenagers, all Christians; and a public open-admissions college serving a very diverse population of adults of all ages from varied socio-economic and educational backgrounds. Such consideration and planning permitted a genuine synergy to emerge when the groups met for the first time and explored WAC topics together in a workshop setting. Beaumont, Pydde, and Tschirpke "strongly agree with the author's suggestion to take time at the beginning of a collaboration and acknowledge each other's experiences and realities. In fact, we experienced that omitting this step can lead to miscommunication and misunderstandings as we describe in Chapter 7" (Chapter 7).

CONTEXT: TWO DIFFERENT SCHOOLS—ONE SHARED INTEREST

When Summit Christian Academy began a writing initiative, one of their history instructors, Ruth, remembered her WAC experiences as an adjunct at a nearby college, Metropolitan Community College-Longview (MCC-Longview). She contacted her administrators and suggested they request support from the WAC Program at MCC-Longview at the outset of their writing initiative. Next, Ruth initiated contact with the WAC director at the college. Within a few months and several dozen emails, Summit Christian Academy (SCA) and MCC-Longview were positioned to pilot a relationship over student writing.

Shared interest quickly morphed into the kind of shared inquiry described by Danielle Lillge in her discussion of secondary WAC as a resource for supporting Common Core State Standards (CCSS): "As teachers struggle with how to meet CCSS expectations, WAC advocates can invite them to the table by considering their pressing questions" (6). Though SCA was not seeking to subscribe to CCSS, they were eager to understand how best to support the writing initiative they had already developed. They had pressing questions about reasonable expectations of teachers, students, and parents, as well as questions about addressing error and cultivating critical thinking through writing.

Those pressing questions were a wonderful way to begin the conversation. However, because context is key in all aspects of WAC, it is important to understand these questions within the curricular context in which they arise. Moreover, on the front side of any WAC collaboration, it is essential to take into account the specific context of each school. These two schools are located within a few miles of each other in Lee's Summit, Missouri, a suburb on the southeast edge of the Kansas City metropolitan area. Prior to this experience, they had little by way of a formal connection, though some SCA graduates attend MCC-Longview. It only took one person with a tie to both schools to forge the connection.

In his essay "Whistling in the Dark," Merrill J. Davies asserts the value of secondary and college English teachers in the same geographic area finding ways to communicate regularly in order to better mitigate the gap between high school and college writing experiences. He suggests that such dialogue would benefit both groups of faculty as they grapple with articulating what constitutes college-level writing. His idea can and should be broadened to apply to instructors across the disciplines as well, because such conversations about writing would otherwise be unlikely to occur.

Initially, there was some hesitation and even a small amount of trepidation on the part of those responsible for the WAC Program at MCC-Longview. The prospect of responding to the request for support from SCA by offering even basic WAC professional development to an audience of middle school and high school teachers seemed daunting on a number of levels. The primary concerns emanated from the sensitivity the community college personnel had about their limited knowledge of teaching at K-12 levels.

In their *WAC Journal* article "Building Better Bridges: What Makes High School-College WAC Collaborations Work?" Jacob Blumner and Pamela Childers note patterns of such collaborations which show that successful relationships between schools must involve "joint commitments," whereby schools *seek* to work together (93). If joint commitments don't exist, misunderstood agendas can undermine all of the best intentions. They explain that a frequent complaint of secondary school teachers is that "university people want to 'come down' and tell them how to teach writing" (94). Community college personnel are acutely aware of this phenomenon from a slightly different perspective, one that reflects their position in the education universe sandwiched between high schools and four-year colleges. Because they operate from primarily a teaching-focused rather than a research-focused mission, community colleges can be caught in a similar predicament in their relationships with four-year institutions, especially if key features of the two-year college setting and curriculum are not fully understood.

Myelle-Watson, Spears, Wellen, McClellan, and Peters (Chapter 5) state:

> As researchers at a public high school in Illinois, we discovered a substantial advantage in having an experienced high school faculty member who could act as a colleague and a liaison to help build bridges and establish joint commitments between our institutions. The National Writing Project model of "teachers teaching teachers" resides at the heart of such an arrangement so that a difference of perspectives and missions do not get mistaken as symptoms of an unhelpful hierarchy. (Peters)

It was precisely this concern that caused those affiliated with the MCC-Longview WAC Program to want to be certain that they were equipped to offer what SCA was seeking. Follow-up questions asked of the SCA administrative contact person to clarify their purposes and goals quelled fears rather quickly, though it wasn't really until the teachers met face-to-face in the WAC workshop that all lingering concerns were eradicated.

However, the difference in grade levels was not the only source of concern; the significant differences in missions and student populations made these two schools an unlikely pairing. It is useful to understand just how different these two schools are in terms of demographics and missions. As one campus of a large, multi-campus district serving a metropolitan area, MCC-Longview is a secular, public, two-year institution with an enrollment of approximately 6000 students that serves the Lee's Summit suburban community. Like most community college environments, MCC-Longview offers both general education and vocational curriculums for a wide range of adult learners, including those who have just exited high school, as well as those returning to school after years away, and often with substantial work and family responsibilities. Student skill levels range from developmental to honors, and student goals and reasons for attending college are quite diverse.

By contrast, Summit Christian Academy is an independent, nondenominational Christian school serving over 685 preschool through high school students. It is accredited both through the North Central Association and the Association of Christian Schools International. The school boasts a 13:1 student-teacher ratio, and has a stellar reputation in the Kansas City area. SCA is noted for its academic rigor and offers 46 college-credit hours each year to high school students; in 2011, SCA graduates averaged a score of 25.2 on the ACT. In addition to pursuing a writing emphasis, the school has embraced a technology initiative. Google Chromebooks and interactive whiteboards have been provided to elementary classrooms, and individual iPads are a required school supply for high school students.

SCA's mission is "to inspire students to achieve their God-given potential through excellent academics and Christian training in a compassionate environment" (Summit Christian Academy, Mission Statement). The school teaches from a biblical worldview, and seeks "to prepare students spiritually, morally, socially, and academically, so they will grow in grace and the knowledge of God and affect their world for Christ" (Summit Christian Academy, Our Mission and Philosophy).

Cox and Gimbel point out in their article on secondary-college WAC collaborations that "college and university WAC programs are uniquely positioned to offer local school districts support in developing and sustaining WAC programs" (3). They are absolutely correct, as long as a joint commitment underpins the relationship. The common ground SCA and MCC-Longview found was their mutual dedication to providing exceptional educational experiences for their students through writing. Both schools were passionately committed to graduating critical thinkers who were confident in their writing skills, and this bond diminished any differences that existed in missions and constituencies and ultimately provided the necessary foundation for fruitful collaboration.

Though common ground and mutual aims are paramount, so too is the assumption that both groups stand to gain insight and knowledge through their partnership and collaboration. Henry A. Luce explains that "collaboration between the sectors, then, becomes the means for bridging the gap between high school and college, for ensuring the continuity of excellence throughout the system (129). Although he wrote his article "High School-College Collaboration," over twenty years ago, his further point resonates even more deeply now: "So if American education is to improve to the extent now demanded by public and private sectors alike, then collegiality must become the most natural act of all" (Luce 129).

BACKSTORIES: THE PATH TO COLLABORATION

In addition to the demographic and mission context, it is helpful to consider specifically each school's writing context. Schools just beginning a writing initiative or WAC program don't always recognize the complex ways writing exists in a school setting, because they focus solely on where writing instruction takes place in the curriculum. Also, schools sometimes overlook activities and endeavors that reflect WAC principles and practices, because they fall outside of language arts instruction. In this case, SCA had already dedicated itself to a focus on writing in order to enhance the college-readiness of their graduates, improve test scores of their students, and directly engage their broader community of teachers and parents to support the development of their students as writers and critical thinkers. Beaumont, Pydde, and Tschirpke (Chapter 7) comment:

> The importance of considering the writing context of collaborating institutions cannot be emphasized enough. Fostering communication about each specific writing culture helps collaborating partners to shed light on potentially deviant writing practices that, when unnoticed, make it difficult to design writing programs that are acknowledged and supported by all collaborating parties equally. (Herkner)

With those goals in mind, the school had adopted a grading procedure that applied to students beginning in January of their junior year of high school and held them accountable for editing papers for which rough drafts were produced. The grading policy covered content, organization, grammar, and mechanics. The administration created a FAQs document explaining the policy that was distributed to teachers and parents. The policy encouraged students to consult resources, like peers, teachers, handbooks, and parents, and included the opportunity to revise for credit. The school also used Turnitin.com for seventh to twelfth grades as a tool for detecting plagiarism. By the time SCA and MCC-Longview connected, the SCA school community was familiar with the grading policy and accustomed to submitting student work to Turnitin. SCA had also integrated a comprehensive literacy program into the elementary grades that encouraged critical reading and analysis of written texts.

In contrast, the WAC Program at MCC-Longview began in 1986 and has since been considered a best practices model of WAC for community colleges. The primary goal of the program has always been to support faculty directly in their efforts to integrate writing into their courses as a tool for learning, and to provide significant writing experiences for students beyond the composition curriculum. To those ends, the program offers introductory WAC workshops for faculty, follow-up workshops for faculty interested in teaching writing intensive courses, a myriad of kinds of forums to foster campus-wide discussion of writing-related topics, and individual consultations for instructors led by a full-time WAC director. Faculty participants had a long history of engaging fully in writing assessment efforts from design to implementation, including a large-scale portfolio project that captured authentic artifacts from courses across the college. Faculty members were able to access the WAC program in multiple ways and determine their own level of involvement, which was entirely voluntary. The program had sponsored a writing fellows program for fifteen years that attached peer tutors to WAC courses, and had hosted a student project showcase event, Imagination Longview, for the past five years.

Just a few months prior to the email query from SCA, MCC-Longview offered a comprehensive, three-day learning experience for new WAC directors called the WAC Institute for Community Colleges. The desire to develop and host such an experience arose during the celebration of the 25th year of MCC-Longview's WAC program when faculty attached to the program and cognizant of the institutional and administrative support the program had always been afforded, wanted to give back by helping other colleges create a blueprint for a sustainable program. The WAC director, along with the WAC Cadre, a representative, interdisciplinary group of WAC faculty who helped guide the MCC-Longview WAC Program, spent considerable time over an 18-month period planning and implementing the WAC Institute, which drew attendees from across the country. They wanted to stress practical strategies that could guide any community college program and decided to do so through the lens of the theme, "Creating a Culture of Writing: What Works."

What is crucial to note is that this effort represented a unique opportunity for some high-level professional development for veteran WAC faculty, as well as for the WAC director. None of them had ever been involved in creating a WAC program from the ground up, because all had joined the Longview community after its WAC Program was established and flourishing. The planning of the institute was based on the idea of honoring all situations that drove interest in WAC at the attendees' colleges, whether it was a full-fledged institutional commitment to a QEP, an administrative mandate, or the interest of a few faculty members to help students write more effectively. And, importantly, this endeavor and approach required each of those involved in this planning to reexamine the fundamental features of thriving WAC programs from the point of view of starting from scratch and assuming limited resources. Consequently, the instructional content of the institute emphasized the decision-making processes attendant to WAC programs, strategies for prioritizing program goals and creating reasonable expectations, and concrete ways to engage faculty and identify administrative allies.

The WAC Cadre had become extremely facile in serving as resources to their peers at MCC-Longview, and especially at helping facilitate WAC and Writing Intensive workshops. But the success of the WAC Institute bolstered their confidence and heightened their awareness of how to communicate broader WAC ideas to colleagues from other institutions. This, in turn, positioned them to serve in a similar role with SCA by helping the school take its writing initiative to the next level, shifting from a culture *emphasizing* writing to a true culture *of* writing.

Finally, proximity alone invites such collaborations. Cox and Gimbel note in Chapter 2 that "too often, educators are separated by level and by discipline." The narrow universe that educators typically work in is organized in ways that can limit exposure to and contact with other disciplines and other grade levels; teachers tend to meet those primarily on their own campus, and attend conferences with those in their own discipline. Creating a WAC community of teachers within driving distance of each other could have huge implications for their teaching and for student learning as the students move from one segment of the educational system to the next.

MAKING CONNECTIONS

Logistics

The initial emails were critical in establishing the relationship between the schools; there was a lot of discussion to try to nail down the details of when and where. One consideration when working with K-12 faculty is timing, both in terms of when during the school year the teachers are available, and at what time of day. MCC-Longview and SCA negotiated the optimum time first based on SCA's available in-service days that could be dedicated to WAC workshops, and then to accommodate the MCC-Longview teacher availability. A second consideration is location. It was clear at the outset that having SCA faculty come to MCC-Longview campus was the best option, because it meant that WAC instructors from across the college would be available to help facilitate around their class schedule. Another advantage of going to the college campus was that the high school teachers were distanced from the everyday distractions at their own school. Myelle-Watson, Spears, Wellen, and Peters (Chapter 5) state:

> Such logistics can be contingent upon a number of factors. When Northern Illinois University tried to host high school faculty in a similar way, the high school faculty soon lost interest in sacrificing their Saturdays to workshops. The best results came from university faculty going to the high school on a mutually convenient weekday, where professors saw firsthand the conditions and exigencies that existed in the teachers' professional lives. Yet there is still a lot for all participants to learn from site visits that go both ways, as McMullen-Light later suggests. (Peters)

Another key logistical decision was to have the high school teachers attend one day and the middle school teachers attend the following day for the first WAC workshop in October. This separation allowed them to work with colleagues who were teaching at similar grade levels for their initial WAC exposure, something that is never necessary to consider at the college workshops. However, for the second workshop in the spring, both middle school teachers and high school teachers attended the half-day session, but worked primarily in discipline-based groups, which permitted vertical planning and course content discussions. This strategy proved particularly effective, as both sessions yielded full and active participation.

Splitting the SCA faculty into two groups permitted the workshops to be conducted in a way that allowed maximum engagement and interaction, especially in the large group setting, where conversations are critical to the efficacy of the workshop.

Planning

In order to develop suitable and relevant materials for the workshops, the WAC director and the WAC Cadre at MCC-Longview spent time discussing the plethora of activities and exercises they had developed and used previously in WAC workshops with college faculty and in the WAC Institute with WAC directors. It was this decision-making process and the desire to match materials to the needs and interests of the SCA teachers that provoked valuable discussion and cultivated new insights regarding WAC theory and practice for the planners. For instance, the WAC Cadre determined that an assignment critique exercise featuring a hypothetical college learning community course typically used in the MCC-Longview WAC workshops wouldn't work as well with the K-12 teachers, because it assumes conditions that don't exist at lower levels. Instead, they developed an assignment design exercise that invited interdisciplinary teams of teachers to generate an assignment in response to a more credible scenario (Appendix A).

WAC Workshop I

The first workshop was an all-day session in October and covered traditional WAC topics, like assignment design principles and strategies for responding to and evaluating student writing. The day included a mix of informational presentations on WAC, small group activities and discussions, large group discussions, responding to scenarios, collaboratively creating assignments and rubrics, writing and sharing individual responses, and viewing the brief film *Shaped by Writing*, produced by Harvard's writing program. Other unplanned conversations naturally related to writing emerged throughout the day, especially because the SCA teachers were instructors keenly interested in how college instructors view and use writing. Seeing actual college assignments and real student responses inspired animated discussions of writing expectations among all present.

WAC Workshop II

The second session took place in February and was designed to revisit ideas related to responding to student writing, giving SCA instructors an opportunity to get collegial feedback on any projects they brought to the table. The session began with a review of how to respond to student writing by using the heuristic of higher order and lower order concerns. After viewing the film *Across the Drafts: Students and Teachers Talk about Feedback*, also produced by Harvard's Writing Program, participants read and analyzed two college student texts and brainstormed how to provide useful feedback to students and best communicate with students to encourage revision. The second half of the session was spent brainstorming any ideas/strategies/projects the teachers had brought with them with the intent to solicit peer feedback, using a tool called "WAC Chat: A Guide to Collegial Conversations," designed to maximize each group's time (Appendix

B).

One SCA teacher described the powerful impact both of these sessions had on her, noting it was "unlike any in-service I have ever experienced." She said she was struck by the way the first session started with everyone seated at tables arranged in a circle, with all participants making eye contact and conversing, taking in information, applying the ideas, sharing personal insights in different ways, moving in and out of small groups, and watching the films.

Though more difficult to arrange with colleagues who are not on your own campus, follow-up sessions ensure impact and ownership (Cox and Gimbel, Chapter 2). Having SCA teachers come to MCC-Longview twice gave the high school teachers an opportunity to apply the strategies they had learned and reflect on their effectiveness. The conversations were decidedly more pointed and specific at Workshop II.

Writing Center Consultation

After the first workshop, SCA's academic dean invited MCC-Longview's WAC director to consult with key staff about the possibility of creating a writing center. Having directed a writing fellows program, the director felt comfortable sharing information about the value of peer tutoring, tutor selection and training, desirable center space and arrangement, and useful resources and materials in an on-site meeting. The WAC director framed a brief set of guiding questions to assist SCA personnel in prioritizing considerations related to creating a writing center in a secondary school (Appendix C).

In "The Natural Connection: The WAC Program and the High School Writing Center," Joan Mullin and Pamela Childers explain that since high school writing centers are able to involve all of the stakeholders—students, teachers, administrators, and even parents—they "can create community support for curricular change in ways often unavailable to universities (24). Once the key SCA staff and administrators made their initial logistical decisions about how the writing center could be set up to support SCA's WAC efforts, student and parent input was sought to ensure that the center could effectively and efficiently serve all constituents.

IMPACTS

SCA Teacher Perceptions from Surveys

During the final minutes of the second workshop, teachers completed a written survey asking them to assess their professional development experiences.

Overall, responses were quite positive and very much in sync with what MCC-Longview instructors convey after workshop experiences, and what other WAC programs typically report about their faculty. Some of the questions are listed below with a smattering of representative comments:

Did you find the WAC workshops worthwhile?

> "Yes, I enjoyed seeing colleagues enthusiastic about a topic that is promised to generate more work."

> "I appreciated the opportunity to 'check in' with other teachers and identify with their joys and frustrations. I feel that I benefitted in some practical and philosophical ways."

> "Yes, totally made writing relevant and helped give me confidence in all aspects of trying to initiate."

Which topic of the workshops was most beneficial to you and why?

> "Light bulb moment: It should have been obvious, but it had not occurred to me to put the majority of my effort as the teacher/evaluator into responding to drafts. I spent a goodly amount of time writing intently to my students' final products, but really it makes far more sense to use that effort in a draft that they'll actually pay attention to later (and conference about). —critical use of technology—which tasks are better suited to it, and which are not."

Would you recommend this workshop (one or both sessions) to your colleagues at other K-12 schools? Why or why not?

> "Yes – practical tools; stuff relatable and took fear out of writing; multidisciplinary staff helpful in seeing possibilities across curriculum."

> "Yes. It was helpful in terms of explaining the writing process and evaluation for non-English teachers."

> "Yes—it has been very encouraging and could be a help to others."

> "Absolutely! The balance of inspiration and practicality was superb. I left feeling, 'I can do this!'"

"Yes. Writing encourages higher level thinking. If students are not able to think critically, they won't do as well in college."

Impact: SCA Teacher Perceptions from Interviews

At the end of the school year, SCA teachers were invited to share their perceptions about the impact of WAC on their pedagogy and the SCA teaching community. The teachers interviewed acknowledged that they saw positive impacts on their teaching and on student learning, and some shared plans for next year, as well as changes they had incorporated this year. Some teachers were interviewed individually and some in a small group.

Ruth, Tenth-Grade History

When asked if she had incorporated an idea or strategy from the workshops or from discussions with SCA or MCC-Longview colleagues, she responded, "I can't begin to tell you how many ideas and strategies I've been inspired to incorporate following WAC workshops. In many ways, it's been overwhelming to consider all of the possibilities. I felt like I was trying to take a drink from one of those giant hoses firefighters use to battle skyscraper blazes."

She then shared her strategy for constraining that vast universe of possibilities:

> Getting back to the tyranny of the immediate in the classroom, I quickly realized I'd have to start by taking three steps: 1) being more aware of whether or not I was giving students multiple opportunities to use writing as a way of thinking, of learning material, and as a gauge of their own understanding; 2) teaming up with a colleague in the English department who would be a combination of accountability partner and bridge to increasing the number, variety, and depth of writing students would tackle; 3) and setting time aside this summer to come back to the workshop material and bringing focus and intentionality to the task of weaving writing into my lesson plans and course curriculum spreadsheet.

Myelle-Watson, Spears, Wellen, and Peters (Chapter 5) agree:

> Both the wisdom and the rhetoric this teacher gives voice to reflect the "aha moment" that teachers also experienced in our Illinois project. While intimidating to launch and sustain such a collaborative venture, such an experience can also be

tremendously liberating from a "tyranny of the immediate" (Siskin 29)—which includes so many pressures that isolate from rather than connect teachers to productive professional relationships with their colleagues. (Peters)

Anthony, Ninth-Grade English

Anthony identified one critical shift he made this year in working with his English students after he attended the WAC workshop: expending more energy on assessing and providing critical feedback on drafts, rather than spending that energy on the final product. He realized that the draft represented the best time to "really coach the students." He envisions that next year he will be "more intentional" in working with students on their drafts by conferencing with them individually over their drafts during class as they obtain peer feedback. The iPads make this a tenable activity, especially if students are working with their assignment checklist in hand. He anticipates shifting his classroom time to accommodate important in-class experiences like this.

He likes that WAC promotes writing in all classes and thinks a consistent expectation level regarding writing is present throughout the school and catching the attention of the students. He has already had conversations with a history teacher about how they can collaborate on projects when he teaches Elie Wiesel's *Night* and F. Scott Fitzgerald's *The Great Gatsby*. He was enthusiastic about working with the history teacher to make overt connections between the literary analysis and the historical context, and sees further opportunity for collaboration with this teacher in relation to their overlapping coverage of Greek mythology.

An interesting application of the ideas that surfaced for Anthony through the workshops was a project for the ESL students he teaches. He decided to have the students write in pairs to encourage their collaboration and to provide increased opportunity for conversing. Though the students were a bit frustrated by this exercise, Anthony says it achieved the goal he had in mind: the paired students talked extensively to each other during the process of creating a single paper. It heightened their awareness of key language features and of the writing process. He stressed that the final draft wasn't nearly as important as the consistent communication that occurred throughout its development. He plans to repeat this project in the fall.

Anthony is still thinking about what he learned through WAC, especially as it plays out against the reality of teaching high school. He wonders about striking that appropriate balance between valuing the ideas and the "grammar piece." He realizes this is an essential topic for discussion next year with his colleagues.

Thomas, Twelfth-Grade English and Dual-Credit

Thomas presently teaches twelfth-grade English, dual credit courses, and online college-level composition courses. For him, the impact of WAC was manifest in greater collegiality, and he sees the opportunity for learning groups, collaboration in writing, and common assessment of students as outgrowths of the school's engagement with WAC:

> We have been in the process of upping our writing game over the last year and a half. Every teacher was required to assign an essay per semester in their discipline and the 75% rule regarding grammar was put into force. Now, we are in the process of establishing a writing center and using both teachers and students to staff the center. Additionally, grammar and writing norm workshops are in the works for next year. Teachers I have spoken to are excited and more interested in collaboration and WAC assignments than they have ever been before.

Tom will be released from some of his teaching load to coordinate the writing center and from that vantage, will encourage the cross-discipline projects other teachers are creating and begin collecting assignments and rubrics to help the peer tutors understand the assignments they will be working with. He will also offer mini-workshops, called "Grammar Slammers," for his colleagues to help them clarify and troubleshoot grammar issues.

Ramona, Ninth-Grade-Science

Diane, Tenth-, Eleventh-, Twelfth-Grade Science

Donna, Middle School Science

Three Science teachers gathered in a conference room at SCA at the end of the school year to share their observations and plans related to WAC:

They plan to meet over the summer to formalize some of their vertical planning which began during the follow-up WAC session at MCC-Longview in the spring. There, in the discipline brainstorming sessions, they spent time identifying writing projects and genres that serve their varying levels of instruction. These and other "eye-opening" conversations led them to discover much more about what other science teachers were doing at other grade levels. For example, one of the high school teachers was surprised to learn that a lower grade teacher had been sending students to the local science fair. They see their collaboration as colleagues as an opportunity to coordinate and build on all of the science experiences SCA students have.

They plan to visit MCC-Longview in the fall to re-connect with Keet, the Biology instructor who facilitated their brainstorming session where they began their vertical planning and observe the lab setting context in which he has his students write.

Some of the changes they instituted this year as they became engaged in WAC:

Donna mentioned that she had set up next year's units to include one writing day per unit, approximately every ten days. On this day, her students will focus on writing and gain experience in several genres relevant to science, including summary, compare and contrast, and creating definitions. Students will have opportunities to use iPads for in-class research, which will be included in one-paragraph write-ups they will produce during class. She gave a sample prompt: What is aquaculture and what are its costs and benefits?

Donna came away from this school year believing that students felt more relaxed and less tense about the prospect of writing; she attributes her integration of informal assignments as the key to taking the fear out of writing for the students. She says, "For some, the writing became more inviting and they could see that they got more out of it." She watched the in-class paragraphs become more focused over the year, and she believes informal assignments like these were "more organic" and "allowed students to put their thoughts down and to focus on learning the science."

Ramona said that her mindset had shifted significantly and that writing had not at all been the burden she'd feared it would be. She offered the example of having her ninth-grade students watch a documentary on Nikolai Tesla and write a brief informational report using only ideas gleaned from the film. She issued a rubric with the assignment via the iPad, and was quite pleased with the student performance on this task. She felt the writing was clear. She had no plagiarism issues because students were acknowledging the ideas they used from the film, and the students were far more invested in their viewing of the film because they knew they would be using it as a source. From her perspective, this exercise yielded "strong writing and better learning."

Diane teaches anatomy and physiology and asked her students to write their notes by hand. She is sold on the value of the kinesthetic experience of writing and received positive results by having students create their notes this way, which was a challenge, given the iPad initiative. She says there is a temptation for students to default to rote memorization if she issues PowerPoint notes. She believes their fundamental understanding of symptoms, causes, and science terminology in this course is enhanced by this approach. Interestingly, very recent research on college students and the positive impact of handwriting course notes (Mueller and Oppenheimer) was mentioned during the first workshop.

Greg, Eleventh- and Twelfth-Grade History

According to Greg, "There are natural conversations occurring between teachers, especially about prospective collaborations." He says they are tweaking assignments and even exploring ways to work around classes that include both juniors and seniors when they seek to devise grade-specific writing experiences. Here's how he knows that the topic of writing is becoming more organic: "Around the lunch table or at the copy machine, teachers used to ask each other, 'How're your kids?' or 'How are the Royals doing?' Now it's become more normal to ask about your writing assignments."

A Conversation:

Around the conference table, this conversation about the effect of WAC on their teaching community emerged:

History (Greg): "The more cohesive faculty become, the less opportunity there is for students to play one teacher against another."

History (Ruth): "This school-wide approach rescues us from the tendency to say my little classroom is my world and not consider the larger context."

Science (Ramona): "Without WAC, it always made the English teacher look like the bad guy."

English (Andrea): "WAC lets the English classroom expand and explore even more because other classes are supporting these ideas."

History (Ruth): "Also, I would not have had the confidence to tackle some of the assignments without the support of the English composition teachers."

English (Andrea): "I found enjoyment in working with colleagues. It can get lonely in your own room."

The high school teachers also pointed out natural connections that could be made to the literacy program that SCA offers at the elementary levels, which focuses on critical reading and analysis. They planned to consult with elementary teachers for strategies to cause students to review the skills they learned in this program, and apply them overtly to discipline-specific reading at the high school level.

Reflections by MCC-Longview WAC Cadre members

The MCC-Longview instructors responded to an email interview after the second session to capture their perspectives as facilitators. The interview prompts focused exclusively on the second workshop, but insights that emerged in meetings and discussions throughout the year signaled that the connection with SCA represented a valuable and worthwhile experience on a number of levels for the WAC Cadre members.

Matthew, Psychology instructor

Matthew first explained how the teachers at his table responded to the task of evaluating the two student papers:

> Our focus was on the Hierarchy of Concerns and how difficult it is to stay high on the list when reading papers with multiple lower level concerns. I suggested reading with empty hands—no correcting pen, in order to focus on the ideas rather than allowing one's self to be distracted by spelling or sentence errors. There was debate over which paper needed more revision, and what types of revision, how meeting with the students to discuss their papers would go. We talked about whether one type of error, done repeatedly through the paper was really one error or multiple, and how to count it.
>
> The discussion of justifying the points subtracted from a perfect score, and writing enough comments to show the reason for the subtraction, was topic. There's the trap of only showing what is wrong because that's all the teacher has to justify, leaving any compliments or strengths unmentioned. It's no wonder students don't like to write, or receive their papers back.

As expected, each group responded differently to the WAC Chat Exercise, tailoring it to the needs of those present around the table. In describing how his group handled the WAC Chat exercise, Matthew explained:

> Our group took turns giving and getting feedback. One member had to leave early, so another chimed in that she really wanted his feedback because they teach the same subject, though at different grade levels. This collegiality was great to see and foster.
>
> Another wanted feedback on a rather complex, multi-part assignment examining culture, language, history, etc. We considered the timing of parts, rather than doing a group assignment, because the ability to do each part was one of the goals for the students. We ended up talking about spacing segments over the semester, so it wasn't overwhelming to students to receive it all at once. I referred back to Cathy's music appreciation assignment, which the faculty member then recalled from the first workshop session in October, and

> we talked about her connecting with Cathy for brainstorming or other ideas.
>
> Another instructor wanted brainstorming and problem solving with a combined English/history paper. She wanted to provide students with one grade for the paper, jointly arrived upon by both instructors. There were several questions before any advising, which was good to see. It ended up with encouragement to try, and let the students know they are experimenting, and that if it doesn't work the way they want it to, they'll change the grading process. Most couldn't see how to make it a single grade, but that it was worth experimenting with."

In terms of his overall impression of the engagement with SCA teachers, Matthew shared this:

> What surprised me at this session and at the original workshop in October was the way the Cadre performed. I had a real concern going into it that we didn't have specific things to say, or points to make, but it turns out we didn't need to because we have been so embedded in WAC for so long that we can be fluid in responding to questions or needs.
>
> I was also very impressed with the creativity, depth, complexity, and appeal of the assignments I heard these faculty present. There were many moments I found myself wanting to either participate or copy. The assignments were intriguing and should help meet the educational goals they have established.

Unquestionably, his comments reflect a veteran WAC instructor's deep understanding of the concepts presented and applied at the workshop sessions.

Anne, Physics Instructor

Anne writes of the collegial brainstorming the teachers at her table engaged in, and offered the example of a sixth-grade history teacher who had prepared for the exercise by bringing student work to share, but seemed reticent about bringing it up to the group, thinking that it wasn't as deep or important as some of the other assignments the group had considered:

> We collectively convinced her that she began the foundation for future work and we were interested. She has her students journal about being on a wagon train. Her project is very realistic in that if it doesn't happen at that period in history then they

aren't going to do it. Historical records show that ten percent of
the people died during their journey, so she has 10% pretend
to die during the journaling about the journey. They have
various hardships along the way and have to overcome those.
They hit key places and times in history and journal about that.
Her questions centered around whether she is doing enough
and what else she could add. I think the upper grade history
teachers were impressed with her work—they really validated
what she was doing. They actually had a hard time giving her
any new ideas. The one idea that they came up with was taking
a class sharing and instruction time and becoming the Indians
around a campfire and telling the events and histories.

Another brainstorming success occurred when a dual credit government teacher sought a way to create a meaningful assignment combining current events with Articles of the Constitution. Anne recounts the discussion:

He said that it sounded like a good idea but most times it
ended up dry and uninteresting (my words, not his but that
is the gist). He wanted ideas that would liven up his class.
We suggested he ask the students to become Supreme Court
justices and write briefs on the current events using the Constitution; we suggested they may also become lawyers arguing
in the Supreme Court, or become legislators trying to get a
bill made into law about these current events; or compare our
constitution with another country's and see how the current
event would look based on the two different constitutions.
It seemed like he was pleased with the ideas and it gave him
the opportunity to think about it in a new light and come up
with some of his own ideas, too.

Anne summarized her experience as a facilitator:

I was really pleased that the sixth-grade teacher went away
with some validation of her project when she initially felt
intimidated by topics of the first person in the group. I also
think the last teacher to share didn't think he'd get any good
ideas, but I could see the slight surprise on his face when
we started giving him some fresh ideas. I think those two
things—validation and fresh ideas—are some of the best
things that can happen when teachers share their ideas, desires
for objectives, and projects. Having others with a teacher's

perspective but little direct knowledge and no personal involvement look at your work can really strengthen the project.

Again, a seasoned WAC teacher is in a unique position to guide other teachers and not only fully appreciate the value of collegial feedback, but also orchestrate a conversation so that it can occur.

Cathy, Music Instructor

Cathy facilitated a table of music and arts teachers who had no trouble generating rich and productive discussion of assignment possibilities. Cathy reported that there was "so much exchange that we ran out of time." She further writes:

> It was so exciting to see the engagement of Longview folks with SCA. I was looking for ideas as much as the SCA art/music faculty. The choir teacher needed some ideas for developing the historical context for music. I suggested the Time Period project we used in Music Appreciation. She is going to adapt it for use in her concerts. For instance, she will have students develop a digital collage around the context of a particular piece of music and present it to the audience during a concert. All kinds of things were discussed—everything from performance art to poetry slams. The art, drama and music faculty had no lack of things to talk about. They have a fully-developed collegial relationship.

In discussions at meetings after both sessions, all of the WAC Cadre members indicated that they had felt invigorated by these sessions and had come away from them with solid ideas they planned to incorporate in their own teaching. One of the most poignant and quite unexpected elements of the workshops that touched these college instructors was the profound way in which the spirituality of the SCA teachers so naturally marked their discussions of their pedagogy and the ideas they shared in this context.

Writing Center Update

Mullin and Childers note that "no writing center or WAC program can be simply lifted from one institution and used successfully in another; it must be adjusted to each school's objectives and demographics" (25). To that end, SCA spent the spring semester designing a plan for a writing center that suited their ongoing writing initiative and WAC. At the end of the school year, the academic dean reported that critical space had been identified and dedicated as the location of the new writing center, to be staffed by ten student tutors, called Writing Fellows, who would be supervised by two teachers to cover both before and after school times. One of the teachers would be released from a class to coordinate the center when it opens the following year.

The Writing Fellows are excited to be the first at SCA to serve in the role of writing tutors. They met as a group and determined the name of the center: The Writer's Corner. The Writing Fellows also chose a Scripture foundation from 1 Corinthians 14:33, *King James Version*: "For God is not the author of confusion, but of peace ..." The dean explained that the Writing Fellows wanted every student to remember that they didn't have to be stressed when writing, "that it would all come together." Clearly, the students involved already have ownership of the idea as well as the space since they have imagined it having a coffee-shop atmosphere-replete with a Keurig coffee machine.

Chad E. Littleton lays out the benefits of shared training between the college and high school writing centers and promotes engagement with local affiliates of the International Writing Centers Association. The MCC-Longview WAC director identified a comprehensive tutor training opportunity and accompanied SCA staff and writing tutors in August to a valuable, day-long tutor retreat developed and hosted by Kansas City area college writing center directors who gather regularly to support one another professionally. This group, "The Greater Kansas City Writing Center Project," includes writing center directors from area two and four-year colleges and universities who are members of IWCA.

One primary project they have developed is an annual tutor retreat. It is run like a conference, with seasoned student tutors, along with writing center directors from each college, conducting breakout sessions on a wide range of relevant topics offered in various formats. Through mock tutorials, presentations, and discussions, they provide a rich training experience with "writing, role-playing, listening, questioning, observing, and information-sharing" (Luce 134). The participation of both high school and college tutors establishes the authentic "community of writers" that Luce calls for (133). As luck would have it, the keynote speaker and presenter this year was a highly regarded high school writing center expert, Andrew Jeter, founder and coordinator of the Literacy Center at Niles West High School in Skokie, Illinois, who generously shared his expertise with SCA administrators over lunch.

STRATEGIES/RECOMMENDATIONS FOR CREATING A K-12-COMMUNITY COLLEGE CONNECTION

What follows is a set of general, guiding principles for connecting with a high school or community college in your area. This list is by no means exhaustive, but it does convey key strategies for a successful high school-community college connection:

- Reach out to another school in your area and suggest a WAC collaboration based on what each has to offer by way of expertise, and what each is interested in learning from the other school.
- Talk early and often in the process to determine needs, and get a sense of the other institution; consider this part of the relationship (phone, email, text, in person).
- Overcome fear about saying/doing the right thing, because you don't know each other's context; if each institution enters into the partnership in an authentic way, good things will happen.
- Plan for interactions that permit open, honest discussion in a safe environment.
- Give faculty time and space to process and apply ideas beyond the initial professional development experiences.
- Reconnect at a later point to dive deeper into topics covered.
- Negotiate: don't let dictates of school calendars get in the way of getting teachers together; find comfortable and convenient spaces in which to have interactions.
- Don't be surprised when you get much more than you give. Teachers are resourceful and imaginative by trade. The process of putting teachers in touch with WAC enriches everyone.
- Honor the good work going on at both places and be prepared to learn.
- Be collegial and respectful by thinking of concrete ways to express and promote collegiality.
- Make site visits in both directions.
- If you have a WAC Program, consider ways in which planning such experiences can provide significant and valuable professional development for veteran WAC faculty.
- Document all interactions; assess effectiveness through surveys and interviews and other means.
- Develop mechanisms for keeping track of what happens with both schools once connections are established (email, website, blogs, updates, Skype, social media, newsletters).

TEACHER TO TEACHER, SCHOOL TO SCHOOL

Finally, what came out of this successful pilot partnership were vital teacher connections within each school and between the two school environments, enhanced collaborations between disciplines at SCA, vibrant and transformative professional development experiences for all of the participants and facilitators, genuine appreciation of the challenges teachers face at each grade level, openness on the part of all to sharing ideas and resources and providing collegial feedback, and the promise of new beginnings with the launch of the SCA writing center, The Writer's Corner.

WORKS CITED

Blumner, Jacob, and Pamela Childers. "Building Better Bridges: What Makes High School-College WAC Collaborations Work?" *The WAC Journal* 22 (2011): 91–101. Web.

Cox, Michelle, and Phyllis Gimbel. "Conversations Among Teachers on Student Writing: WAC/Secondary Education Partnerships at BSU." *Across the Disciplines* 9.3 (2012). Web. 10 June 2013.

Davies, Merrill. "Whistling in the Dark." *What is "College-Level" Writing?* Eds. Patrick Sullivan and Howard Tinberg. Urbana: NCTE, 2006. 31-35. Print.

Herkner, Luise. "Fwd: Kommentare." Email to Jacob Blumner and Pam Childers. 31 August 2013.

Lillge, Danielle. "Illuminating Possibilities: Secondary Writing Across the Curriculum as a Resource for Navigating Common Core State Standards." *Across the Disciplines* 9.3 (2012). Web.

Littleton, Chad E. "Creating Connections Between Secondary and College Writing Centers." *The Clearing House: A Journal of Educational Strategies, Issues and Ideas*, 80.2 (2006):77-78. Web.

Luce, Henry A. "High School-College Collaboration." *The High School Writing Center: Establishing and Maintaining One.* Ed. Pamela B. Farrell. Urbana: NCTE, 1998. 127-35. Print.

Muller, Pam A., and Daniel M. Oppenheimer. "The Pen is Mightier than the Keyboard: Advantages of Longhand over Laptop Note Taking." *Psychological Science*, 23 (2014). Web.

Mullin, Joan, and Pamela Childers. "The Natural Connection: The WAC Program and the High School Writing Center." *The Clearing House: A Journal of Educational Strategies, Issues and Ideas*, 69.1(1995): 24-26.

Peters, Bradley. "Comment on Chapter 6." Email to Jacob Blumner. 1 September 2013.

Siskin, Leslie. "Subject Divisions." *The Subjects in Question: Departmental Organization and the High School.* Eds. Leslie Siskin and Judith Little. New York: Teachers College P, 1995. 23-47. Print.

Summit Christian Academy. Mission Statement. *Who We Are.* Web. 1 January

2013. <http://www.summit-christian-academy.org/sca-who-we-are.html>.

Summit Christian Academy. Our Mission and Philosophy. *Media Fact Sheet.* Web. 1 January 2013. <http://www.summit-christian-academy.org/sca-media-fact-sheet.html>.

APPENDIX A: ASSIGNMENT DESIGN SCENARIO

A new Department of Secondary Education and Department of Conservation policy has determined that all Missouri high school students will be provided an opportunity to learn about native flora and fauna of the state. This effort is intended to heighten awareness of the environment and can be incorporated into **any** course. There is no expectation of student assessment regarding this experience, but innovative teaching and learning approaches will be showcased in local forums throughout the state.

Choose the grade level and at least two design principles from the list to feature.
Grade Level:
Course(s):
Purpose:
Idea:
Kind of product:
Process/Steps for completion:
Principles to be featured:
Signal if this experience is high stakes or low stakes:

APPENDIX B: WAC CHAT: A GUIDE FOR COLLEGIAL CONVERSATIONS

This exercise affords each group member the opportunity to serve once as an initiator of a discussion and multiple times as a respondent in a discussion. Each initiator should be granted ten minutes of group attention.

As an initiator, you will choose to solicit from your group ONE of three responses:
- feedback on an existing project, rubric, idea, strategy, task, assignment
- brainstorming for a new project, rubric, idea, strategy, task, assignment
- troubleshooting for a problem or concern

INITIATOR-Choose one of these options:

FEEDBACK
Describe in detail the project, rubric, idea, strategy, task, assignment.

BRAINSTORM
   Describe the context of your class (subject, level, learning outcomes).
   Describe any relevant circumstances or conditions.
   Share the idea you want to develop.
TROUBLESHOOT
   Identify the problem or concern.
   Explain any complicating factors.
   Share solutions you have tried thus far.
   As a respondent, you will actively listen to each initiator and respond according to the parameters indicated in the guidelines below.

RESPONDENT-Provide one of the following:

FEEDBACK
   Actively listen to description of project, rubric, idea, strategy, task, assignment.
   Ask questions until you fully understand nature of it.
   Imagine you are a student and consider: what else do you need to know to be successful?
   Is this subscribing to WAC principles of assignment design and evaluation/response ?
BRAINSTORM
   Actively listen to context and conditions shared by initiator.
   Pitch ideas as they occur to you.
   Piggyback onto ideas of others.
   Examine trends if any emerge.
TROUBLESHOOT
   Actively listen to problem presented.
   Survey solutions tried thus far.
   Imagine alternative solutions.
   Offer advice.
   Consider options.
   Poll and pool resources of group: what can you offer your colleague by way of support?

APPENDIX C: WRITING CENTER CONSIDERATIONS

1. **Premises:**
   - All writers benefit from feedback.
   - All writers should learn to be critical readers of their own work.
   - Tutoring is not simply about remediation or editing; it focuses on

supporting the process of writing and revising.
- There are substantial benefits derived from peer-to-peer contact.

2. Logistics
- Where will it be located?
- How will students access it?
- When will students access it?
- What will it be called?
- What will be its services?

3. Staffing

Tutors
- Who are the tutors?
- How will they be selected?
- What are the necessary qualifications?
- What training will be provided and how often?
- What do they receive for serving? (Service hours, credit?)

Faculty
- Who trains tutors?
- Who supervises tutors?
- How is their workload accommodated?

4. Oversight
- Who guides the development of the center?
- Is there a designated director—permanent/rotating?
- Is there a faculty advisory group?
- (an interdisciplinary mix of faculty from different grad levels; some centers include other community stakeholders—parents/business community, etc.)

Connecting to writing center resources-regional/national
- Will they interact/collaborate with nearby WAC-based writing centers at other academic levels?

CHAPTER 7

NEGOTIATING EXPECTATIONS: OVERCOMING OBSTACLES INTRODUCING WAC THROUGH COLLABORATION BETWEEN A GERMAN UNIVERSITY WRITING CENTER AND GERMAN HIGH SCHOOLS

Luise Beaumont, Mandy Pydde, and Simone Tschirpke

The curricula of most German high schools still lack what writing research and writing pedagogy have been postulating for years: teaching and applying writing as a process and as a tool for critical, creative and reflective thinking and learning across subject borders. Instead, writing is widely taught and learned as linear process and applied as an instrument for testing knowledge. The writing process itself is left in a black box, as well as differences between product-oriented and process-oriented approaches to writing. The product-oriented approach is still prevailing in teaching and learning writing (Bräuer 20). In fact, writing activities, apart from the Aufsatzunterricht (essay lessons), mainly focus on transcribing text from a course book, a blackboard or from other text material (Merz-Grötsch 131). Only little or no room is provided for alternative approaches, revision practices, or constructive feedback.[1]

However, some initiatives exist that focus on enriching students' writing experiences by fostering writing as a tool for learning in and across the disciplines. Projects range from writing across the curriculum (WAC) workshops given by academic staff (Micheel and Vogel), to tutoring sessions in writing by university students (Rapp; Schiller), and peer tutoring sessions by high school students for their classmates (Pydde, Tschirpke, and Herkner) —mostly introduced to schools by external writing specialists. From our own experiences and from the experiences of colleagues, we know that such projects struggle mostly with changing the culture of writing on a long-term basis.

In this article, we use the opportunity to look at data we collected throughout our project, *Peer Tutoring and Writing Workshops by High School Students for High School Students*, that focused on establishing student-run high school writing centers as a physical space for WAC activities and peer tutoring in writing. We, as university writing center peer tutors, were appointed to put the project into practice. Because it was not possible to establish sustainable structures, we focused this study on finding reasons for these shortcomings. We assume that the expectations of all participating project partners played an important role in the development and outcome of the program. Our research question for this article, therefore, is as follows: What expectations can arise in a collaboration between high schools and universities, and how did these expectations, if differing, develop? We will analyze our data according to Philipp Mayring's qualitative content analysis using teacher interviews and university tutors' field notes to filter teachers' and university tutors' expectations. We will then present and discuss our findings and give recommendations for similar future projects.

PROJECT "PEER TUTORING AND WRITING WORKSHOPS BY HIGH SCHOOL STUDENTS FOR HIGH SCHOOL STUDENTS"

The idea of bringing writing center practices to high schools grew strong in 2008, when the director of our writing center at the European University Viadrina (EUV), Katrin Girgensohn, wrote a concept for a project that would aim at establishing writing centers at German high schools. As a large part of the belief in successful learning stems from the concept of collaborative learning, it was understood that peer tutoring—as a learning and teaching method—would have to be at the heart of this project. Another reason to choose peer tutoring as our primary working method was that peer tutors are closer to students in terms of age and status. Peer tutors are able to relate to personal experiences, and thus can approach and reach writers differently than teachers (Harris 27). Having only a few years difference between us as peer tutors, as well as being students, we saw ourselves as possible peer tutors to juniors and seniors of the respective high schools.

After the Robert Bosch Stiftung,[2] an institution that grants funding for educational projects, approved the proposal, we started assembling a project team and actively searched for schools to partner with. Three university peer tutors formed the university team and selected schools that either approached us, knew the director of our writing center, or were one of the members of our project team.

In order to find suitable students to educate into peer tutors, we promoted our project among teacher assemblies and went into classrooms to present our program to students. We asked applicants to write a letter of interest and discussed students' participation with their teachers. We then chose three to eight juniors or seniors from each school that showed social competence, commitment, and reliability. These students took part in a three-day training at our university and the writing center. This training took place once every year when a new project cycle with new juniors and seniors began.

In the three-day course, the university team imparted basic knowledge about writing processes, writing strategies, and academic working techniques, which the students practiced and reflected upon.[3] Principles of peer tutoring were elaborated upon and practiced in mock tutorials. A workshop for exploring ideas on how to implement the newly learned peer tutoring processes, strategies, and techniques at the respective schools was one of the most important units at training.

With these objectives, the implicit aims of the project were the following:

- Promote student autonomy;
- Promote collective acquisition of learning content on student level;
- Promote thinking and writing across disciplines;
- Build writing competencies as key competence for educational processes through targeting and linking students' creative likings and individual interests, maximizing the potential of writing as an educational medium at school;[4]
- Transfer research findings (didactics of writing) from university to high school; and
- Familiarize teachers with writing-specific, didactical findings to ensure the establishment of sustainable structures at the respective schools.

After the initial training, two members of the university team met frequently with the student peer tutors at their schools to set up workshops and one-on-one tutoring sessions. During the frequent meetings, we trained and developed the students' peer tutoring skills continuously, and made sure they were able to implement what they had learned. The third member of the university team was responsible for coordinating the project. Due to other commitments and university tutors finishing their degrees, studying abroad, etc., the composition of our team changed multiple times. Only the coordinator stayed with the project for all three years.

Although our team dynamics changed many times, we consistently worked on keeping a strong rapport with our student peer tutors. Our meetings were almost always informal and we held them at our own apartments more than once. We also tried to have many activities that didn't include work, but rather focused on personal writing. We wanted the peer tutors to enjoy writing, and therefore, we went on explorative walks through Berlin, and asked them to document their impressions and write in any form they wanted to. These activities were the basis for making collages and other posters that were hung in their writing center in order to keep them motivated and to attract other students.

Unfortunately, we weren't able to devote the same time and energy to working with the teachers from the respective schools. One of our main concerns in working with the teachers and the board of schools was building a steering committee. We thought that a steering committee, consisting of teachers, parents and us as tutors, would ensure the project's sustainability. We knew that teachers were often at capacity, and we hoped that parents could become engaged and take active roles. Unfortunately, due to limited teacher involvement, we weren't able to form such a committee at any of the three schools.

After three years the project had the following results:

- Twenty-one high school students were trained and became peer tutors;
- High school peer tutors offered individual writing consultations;
- Thirty individual writing consultations were held;
- High school peer tutors gave multiple workshops;
- Social competence of high school peer tutors was nurtured through inter-year collaboration with peers;
- Writing competence of high school peer tutors, as well as some peers, was further developed;
- Writing centers and ongoing peer tutoring could not be established;
- One school wanted to continue peer tutoring by training a teacher that functions as trainer for future student peer tutors; and
- Teacher commitment was insufficient for establishing sustainable structures at their respective schools.

ANALYSIS OF DATA MATERIAL

Throughout the entire project, the university team compiled notes, reports, and other qualitative material. This material provided crucial information about varying aspects of the work of the project team. In order to filter the multiple expectations participants had, we performed a qualitative content analysis,[5] according to Philipp Mayring,[6] which will be summarized briefly.

Qualitative content analysis integrates elements of hermeneutics and, in general, aims at analyzing text material of every possible origin (Gläser; Flick). There are three types of qualitative content analysis: summary, explication, and structuring (Mayring *Grundlagen und Techniken*). For this study, the summary technique is most important. The large amount of material is gradually reduced, and through methods of abstraction, the central content is extracted.

The qualitative content analysis is a very detailed method of analysis, and is strictly controlled methodologically (Mayring, Grundlagen und Techniken; Mayring, Forum). First, the text is put into the context of its communicational situation. Factors, such as who the author of the text is and the situation in which the piece has been written, play a crucial role (Mayring, Forum). Then, the material is segmented into small units and analyzed step-by-step (Flick; Mayring, Grundlagen und Techniken). The categories for the analysis are developed directly from the material (inductive categorization), but the whole analysis process is theoretically controlled. Categories, once developed, are revised constantly during the analytical process (Flick; Mayring, Forum; Grundlagen und Techniken 86). The following chart illustrates the procedure of a summarizing qualitative content analysis (Flick 201f), which was performed in this research:

Table 1: Procedure of a summarizing qualitative content analysis (cf. Flick)

1	Choice of material
2	Analysis of situation of the origin of material
3	Formal characteristics of material
4	Direction of analysis
5	Theoretical differentiation of research question
6	Definition of techniques for analysis and decision on specific model of analysis
7	Definition of analysis units
8	Paraphrasing text parts that contain important content
9	Definition of aspired level of abstraction, generalization of paraphrases under this level
0	First reduction: selection. Elimination of paraphrases with the same meaning
1	Second reduction: grouping. Integration of paraphrases according to aspired level of abstraction
2	Compilation of new statements as a system of categories
3	Revisal of the summarizing system of categories with regard to original material
4	Interpretation of results according to research question
5	Performance of quality criteria concerning content analysis

In order to make our research both transparent and comprehensible, we will shortly summarize the individual steps we took when performing Mayring's qualitative content analysis.

The project was assessed by Gerd Bräuer, the external evaluator who supported us in terms of choosing training methods for students, collaborating with teachers, and communicating with the Bosch foundation. One particular piece of advice he gave us was to write field notes in order to capture our work and to reflect on it on a continual basis. Accordingly, an extensive amount of protocols accumulated over the three years of the project. Additionally, one member of our team interviewed teachers who were involved in the project shortly after it ended.

In order to answer the main question of this article concerning the expectations of the different participants in the project, we decided to focus on the following material for the perspective target group:

Table 2: Material chosen for qualitative content analysis

Expectations of university team	Field notes from various team members
Expectations of teachers	Interview transcripts

Only members of the university team wrote field notes. Each member took notes individually whenever it seemed necessary or helpful. The following questions structured these notes:

- Documentation of events: What happened? What were the results?
- Analysis of events: Which circumstances led to a positive or negative outcome?
- Evaluation: What surprised you?
- What are the consequences for your future actions?

We circulated our notes with each other at regular intervals, which ensured an exchange of perceptions. As the content of the field notes indicate, this material is oftentimes very personal and subjective. We selected parts of every member's field notes in order to display the perception of the whole team. Protocols that only described the ongoing work, but didn't fit the research question, were not considered for analysis.

The teacher interviews used in this analysis were part of a master thesis that studied teachers' perceptions about the project. Each of the teachers interviewed played a crucial role within the project. It was expected that their responses contained personal evaluations of the project, because each of them answered the questions from memory. The interview questions allowed the teachers to narrate their perceptions, which some did more extensively than others. All interviews were recorded and later transcribed. To ensure an equal presentation of each school and a variety of expectations, we chose one teacher interview per school.

When reaching the last step of Mayring's inductive categorization, we started to compile the statements into a category system. It became evident quickly that we had to let go of the separation of the university teams' statements and the teachers' statements. We originally thought that we would look at the two groups separately and compare the categories of both groups. The material, however, suggested that we look at the statements of the project team in general, because not only did expectations differ between the university team and the teachers, but also within those groups. We found that there was no homogenous group that opposed the other. Rather, the entire project team (consisting of teachers and us) was very heterogeneous and expectations diverged between all participants.

COMMUNICATION, ENGAGEMENT AND CONDITIONS

Having analyzed the data material as described above, a category system was developed that revealed the expectations of the participating parties in the project. The following categories with the corresponding subcategories were formed:

Table 3: Results

Category	Subcategory
1. Communication	1.1 Style
	1.2 Content
2. Engagement	2.1 Responsibility
	2.2 Pro-activeness
	2.3 Continuity
	2.4 Cooperativeness
3. Conditions	3.1 Time
	3.2 Space
	3.3 Finance
	3.4 Structure
	3.5 Administration/staff
	3.6 Legal

It became evident that within the project, the participating parties had different expectations concerning engagement, communication, and the conditions in which the project operated. With this, we mean that participating parties had different expectations concerning how and in what circumstances to work together, and how to communicate with each other. These expectations had an impact on the development of the project and are subsumed accordingly under the categories Communication, Engagement, and Conditions.

First, we want to briefly describe the categories, and then elaborate and illustrate them by providing examples.

Communication

This category summarized university tutors' and teachers' expectations towards their style of communication with each other, as well as the content that was expected to be communicated. We therefore divided this category into the following subcategories: *Style (1.1)*, with the subdivisions *Mutual* and *Respectful*, and *Content (1.2)*, with the subdivisions *Tasks*, *Needs*, and *Assumptions*.

As *Style*, we understood the manner in which communication would take place. *Mutual* highlighted the university team's expectations that all communication would happen in a bilateral understanding. *Respectful* showed that it was expected that all participants would communicate in a manner of respect with each other.

As *Content*, we understood the communication about assignments, tasks, and needs that the project would address and work towards.

According to the collected material, these expectations were mostly addressed by the university team in reference to communication with teachers and high school students. In most cases, members of the university team were surprised about the manner in which communication happened. Those moments of surprise depicted underlying expectations very well, especially about the two subcategories of *Mutual* and *Respectful*. There were, for example, occasions where teachers thought we were high school students and addressed us as such, when we had already worked regularly at the schools. In these situations, two things struck us most: on the one hand, according to our field notes, communication towards students seemed to be rather harsh, impatient and sometimes even disrespectful. On the other hand, it was quite disturbing for us to have to explain our position and authority repeatedly. The atmosphere between teachers and our team could best be described as distant, stressed, and charged, especially due to the style of communication.

The interviews with the teachers also showed that expectations concerning the content of communication differed a lot. There were incidents when teachers felt belittled or not taken seriously when it came to being experts in their fields, especially when it came to student support in the classroom. Our team saw itself as experienced in peer tutoring, setting up writing centers, and WAC, and thus aimed to support and enable teachers to effectively support their high school students both inside and outside the classroom. Meanwhile, teachers expected to effectively distribute tasks and finish meetings sooner rather than later.

Engagement

This category entailed modes of engagement that were anticipated by the participants of the project and was divided into: *Responsibility (2.1)*, *Pro-activeness (2.2)*, *Continuity (2.3)*, and *Cooperativeness (2.4)*.

The subcategory *Responsibility* indicated that it was expected that all participants would feel responsible for the project. The subcategory *Pro-activeness* highlighted expectations about taking active roles in the project. The subcategory *Continuity* subsumed project members' expectations towards the continuity of tasks and the constant engagement with these. It also related to the stability of the project and continuous efforts to establish peer tutoring and a writing center. *Cooperative* engagement described what level of cooperation participants expected from each other.

The different expectations about engagement can best be displayed with our attempt to set up a steering group. This task turned out to be extremely frustrating for all participants. Our team felt alone with this task, and repeatedly got the impression that the teachers' commitment to engage in the project was very poor. Teachers felt continually pressured by us to engage more, and therefore emphasized multiple times how limited their time and resources were, and how difficult it is to change certain aspects in the school structure. Engagement was clearly but very differently defined by all members of the project, and those different assumptions constantly led to misunderstandings, frustrations, and poor results in the ongoing project work.

Conditions

This category related to the fact that all participants, especially our team, had several expectations about the conditions they would be working in and with. This category showed how everyone's expectations relied on outside factors. The classification was developed with the following subcategories: *Time (3.1)*, *Space (3.2)*, *Finance (3.3)*, *Structure (3.4)*, *Administration/Staff (3.5)* and *Legal (3.6)*.

The subcategory *Time* comprised participants' expectations towards handling the limitation of time. From the beginning of the project, all participants were under time constraints. Teachers had little spare time due to limited capacities and full curricula, and our team was continuously at capacity due to unforeseen obstacles that challenged us in ways we did not anticipate.

One of these unforeseen obstacles for our team was how difficult the team-building process and the establishment of basic rules of social behavior amongst the high school students was. We expected the high school students to be at a much higher level concerning communication and team-working skills. The time we originally planned for tutoring the students had to be doubled and still was not enough.

The classification *Space* consisted of our expectations towards the existence of space that we could use for tutoring peers and establishing a writing center. Most schools had very limited space resources, which we did not anticipate. When it came to the challenge of space, it became obvious that the categories of communication and engagement were interlinked. During the process of finding proper space for tutoring and setting up a writing center, communication turned out to be very difficult between teachers and our team. Teachers often felt pressured to deliver a space for the project that in their opinion, was not available. Our team continuously felt urged to emphasize the importance of space for the high school students, because no space became available. Also, the expectations about the engagement to eventually secure this space were very different. Teachers expected our team to be understanding and patient. We, however, expected teachers to be more proactive and creative in making space for the writing center.

The subcategory *Finance* dealt with expectations towards the project's financial situation, entailing mostly our assumptions about financial compensation and financial stability for our work. The expectations were that we would not have to worry about getting paid. Also, the time invested in the project did not represent the salary our team received. Because we needed more time to support the students than we anticipated, we expected our salary to increase proportionally. This, however, did not take place, because funding did not increase. Our financial situation became difficult for the entirety of the project, and repeatedly caused frustration and disappointment.

The subcategory *Structure* comprised expectations towards the structural integration of the project into the school syllabus, and also towards the inner structural conditions of the project itself. After having conducted the first training of high school student peer tutors, and after confronting and dealing with obstacles at the prospective schools, we soon realized that it was necessary for the project to become an integrated component of the school syllabus. At this point, it became very clear that in order to establish peer tutoring in writing, we needed teachers to collaborate. We suggested specific writing assignments that allowed students to work in a process-oriented fashion, and consult with their peer tutors to benefit from the assignments in multiple ways. In doing that, we faced a lot of resistance directly when teachers explained why they could not do what we suggested and justified it with their experience, and indirectly when teachers simply did not give the assignments. It became obvious that we tried to introduce peer tutoring in writing, and at the same time, we tried to establish WAC at the schools. We soon found out that introducing WAC to the schools was an expectation that only university tutors shared. In contrast, the participating schools expected our project to be rather integrated in the structure of our university writing center, and regarded the initiatives as external impulses with no need of integration into school structures.

Finally, the subcategory *Administration/Staff* consisted of expectations towards the availability of teachers and staff at the school, and our team at the university. The sub-group *Legal* encompassed our team's expectations towards legal issues with the project.

Discussion: Service-Oriented vs. Collaborative-Oriented Approach

Looking at the categories that derived from the text analysis, it became evident that diverse expectations among teachers and our team concerning engagement, communication, and various external conditions existed. In fact, we found that expectations concerning the way of how project parties engaged in setting up a student-run writing center, as well as the way parties expected to communicate with each other, can be arranged on a continuum between what we call a service-oriented approach and a collaborative-oriented approach towards the project. These two terms describe very well what kind of expectations project participants had, especially about how to engage in the development of the project, and about how to communicate with other project participants. Before discussing how far the occurrence of both approaches has influenced the development of the project and, indeed, caused several problems, we will look at each approach separately to better understand the underlying concepts.

As a *service-oriented* approach, we understand the expectation of giving or receiving a service. Within the mindset of a service-oriented approach, an individual expects to be on the receiving end of a cooperation. Also, there can be a service-oriented producer who is willing to deliver a service to other cooperating participants. Thus, a service-oriented perspective goes hand-in-hand with a certain expectation on how different parties engage in a project, as well as the way parties communicate with each other. From a service-oriented perspective, engagement is merely thought of as delivering or receiving a service, and communication is thought of as a tool for giving or receiving information. There is no need for in depth exchange, because it is not the goal to create something from the basis of shared knowledge. Rather, it is the goal that each party gives whatever it is they have to offer, and thus a goal can be reached effectively and time efficiently.

In contrast to a service-oriented approach, a *collaborative-oriented* approach entails that a project is steered, developed and pushed forward collaboratively. This means that all participants expect to be in continuous exchange with each other and share responsibilities for the success of the project. From a collaborative-oriented perspective, engagement is seen as an active and responsible participation, and communication is expected to be an exchange and a discussion of ideas from which a consensus is reached. This approach seems to be much more time consuming, because an in depth exchange of knowledge and ideas is essential. Parties who take this approach do not merely want to reach goals in a cooperative manner, but learn from one another and thus, create more knowledge.

The data revealed that among teachers and our team, both approaches and a corresponding set of expectations was found. However, the texts of the analysis suggested the tendency that teachers from the cooperating high schools were more service-oriented, and our team was more collaborative-oriented. On the one hand, this might be explained with writing centers' philosophy that is strongly focused on collaboration and jointly created knowledge. On the other hand, the participating high schools never really owned the idea of setting up a writing center, establishing peer tutoring in writing, and introducing WAC into the school syllabus. Accordingly, there was no room for the participating teachers to interact collaboratively with a project team that would consist of teachers, university tutors, high school students and parents, especially within their normal workload.

The material showed that expectations on both sides ranged from assumptions that all participants take shared responsibility and actively push the project forward, to expecting that the project is a service to the institutions, meaning that some participants expected to have everything handed to them instead of having to work together. The same was noticed when it came to terms of communication. Here, expectations ranged from having a mutual exchange of information, to dictating information without any kind of negotiation.

It is obvious that this mixture of partly conflicting expectations led to frustrations and caused several problems and misunderstandings due to lack of communication and transparency. The following example highlights such a situation: Teachers asked our team to give a workshop for ninth graders who were supposed to submit a short research paper, and the papers had to be submitted on the same day the workshop was held. Due to lack of time from the teachers' side, no collaborative efforts were made concerning the content and structure of the workshop. Hence, all responsibilities (preparation, conduction and reflection of the workshop) stayed with our team and the high school peer tutors.

This example shows that the school outsourced the completion of a task to us without being able to discuss and think through possible workshop designs. In this situation, we took the positions of substitute teachers, which was not a job we had agreed upon or were familiar with. The service expected by the teachers did not match the philosophy of the project. Where our team wanted to focus on process-oriented writing, the teachers expected a "do-it" service within a very short amount of time. As this example shows that teachers tended to take the service-oriented approach, we can use the same example to show that the university team took this approach as well. Instead of communicating to the teacher that this kind of task is against peer tutoring philosophies, we took it on and fulfilled it as best as possible. This occurred many times when teachers asked for workshops. Not once did our team insist on teacher participation when designing workshops. Instead, we hoped that when we delivered the service, the teachers would recognize value and finally engage in the project in general.

Ambivalent expectations also became visible in the following example: A participating school in the project had stated their interest in establishing peer tutoring in writing, because they saw a need in supporting students with their "Facharbeit," which is a short research paper. However, at the same time, the school emphasized that teachers already offer enough guidance within their classes to support students.

In another case, our team had very clear expectations about what was needed in order to establish a student-run writing center, and they expressed and demanded these needs to teachers and deans. Here, we tried to establish a steering group that was supposed to serve the purpose of collaboratively developing and nurturing the project. Yet, such a team never formed, because school administrations and teachers did not see the need for it. Instead of sitting together and discussing possible actions that would be in the interest of all parties, participants were frustrated because their expectations were not met.

Expectations, in fact, often cannot easily be met, because only rarely are they stated explicitly or made transparent. Even more so, expectations influence our actions unconsciously. In order to make expectations visible, we have to actively monitor and reflect our actions. Field notes, protocols, reports, and team meetings are excellent means to reveal underlying dynamics, and can uncover misunderstandings to help minimize frustrations. We also argue that the tasks of monitoring, reflecting, and adjusting actions as well as expectations throughout the course of a project are part of overall project management. Unfortunately, we had no one to fill this position. Instead, the project was poorly staffed, and only a few people had to manage everything.

Apart from that, time was a crucial factor that was missing, because participants rarely sat together and openly spoke about their expectations concerning the project itself. Even though the project team tried to communicate expectations along the way, that very crucial moment of setting the agenda for the project together with school board, teachers and students at the very beginning of the project was not given enough time. This can be explained by the four-month delay with which our team started the project.[7] Because time played a major role from the beginning of the project we constantly worked under a lot of pressure and under the impression that things needed to develop very quickly. This was true for all participants, including the high school students. It was most likely because of these circumstances that all participants started working on practical aspects of the project before aligning a theoretical framework and plan together. Conditions, such as allowing our team to form and learn how to express and negotiate individual expectations in a constructive manner, simply had to be omitted. Thus, the importance of negotiating expectations at the very beginning of the project was clearly underestimated, which we again ascribe to the lack of proper project management.

The qualitative content analysis clearly confirmed our hypothesis that expectations needed to be made visible through transparent communication and sound project management. The analyzed material showed that most of the challenges that occurred throughout the project can be traced to diverging expectations amongst the overall project team. Had these expectations been identified, made transparent, acknowledged and properly negotiated, frustration amongst participants would have decreased profoundly, and the project might have been able to achieve its goals.

RECOMMENDATIONS FOR FUTURE PROJECTS

When we started the project, not much had been published on high school and writing center collaboration in Germany, because only few projects existed. However, considering the current development of writing center work and WAC initiatives, we are optimistic that more projects will be initiated and shared. This will undoubtedly increase our learning opportunities, as we will have more possibilities to gain insight into other projects, learn about best practice examples, and share our experiences.

The following recommendations derive from the experiences we made and might help to negotiate expectations in future projects:

- Make sure all potential participants want to be involved. Often, the school administration is excited about a project, but are the teachers on board?
- Make sure all participants understand the concept of the project and are willing to a) accept and fully support it, or b) negotiate and appropriate it to the different schools.
- Establish rules of communication. This sounds much like teaching school children to respect each other, but when different educational worlds meet, it is absolutely essential that everyone knows what (content), when (in what time span), and how (in what manner) to communicate.
- Take time to sit down and ask teachers, high school students, and the

school administration what their goals and expectations are for the duration of the project, as well as after the project concludes. This seems like an "of-course" fact, but the key is to make time for meetings before you start the project, and to keep these meetings happening during the course of the project.
- Clearly define and negotiate on a regular basis participants' roles in the project (especially if new members are anticipated).
- Document, share, and sign all agreements with all participants to ensure everyone knows and commits to the established rules, etc.
- Establish a steering group that is willing to support your endeavor before any practical steps are taken.
- Decide on tools for documenting and reflecting upon what is happening throughout the project, e.g., through the use of field notes, minutes, and reflections. The purpose of documenting should be made clear to all participants so that everybody understands the importance of those notes. Furthermore, consider how these documents are evaluated throughout the project—they can be very valuable when they are discussed within the project team and decisions are made based on them.

We are aware that the recommendations we give from reflecting on our project are not universally applicable, because every team and every project is different. However, some aspects, especially concerning communication and engagement, are issues that should be addressed whenever trying to establish WAC or a writing center at an external institution.

NOTES

1. At this point it is worth mentioning that schools in general show no collaborative approach to learning when it comes to writing, because there is no exchange of ideas, feedback, etc. between students. Students receive feedback from teachers, which is only given with the final grade.

2. "The Robert Bosch Stiftung is one of the major German foundations associated with a private company and has managed the philanthropic bequest of company founder Robert Bosch for more than forty years. Indeed, it was his entrepreneurial vision, political farsightedness, moral fortitude and charitable initiatives that set the standards for the work of the Robert Bosch Stiftung." (Robert Bosch Stiftung)

3. A more detailed description of the three-day training and the entire project can be found in: "Paving the Way for Writing Across the Curriculum: Establishing Writing Centers and Peer Tutoring at High Schools in Germany" (http://wac.

colostate.edu/atd/second_educ/herkneretal.cfm).

4. As Girgensohn explains insufficient writing competence can often be a reason for failing or even beginning a tertiary education (2).

5. The qualitative content analysis originally emerged from communication studies. It was first developed in the US in the twentieth century as a quantitative research method (Gläser; Mayring). In Germany the Mayring model, developed in the 1980s, is most central when qualitative content analysis is performed (Flick; Gläser).

6. Mayring is a German psychologist, sociologist, and pedagogue, as well as founding member of the qualitative content analysis.

7. The proposal for the project funding suggested a start of the project in the month of June, but funding was only granted in September.

WORKS CITED

Becker-Mrotzek, Michael, and Ingrid Böttcher, eds. *Schreibkompetenz entwickeln und beurteilen.* Berlin: Cornelsen, 2006. Print

Blumner, Jacob, and Pamela Childers. "Building Better Bridges: What Makes High School-College WAC Collaborations Work?" *The WAC Journal* 22 (2011): 91–101.Web.

Bräuer, Gerd. "Plädoyer für einen anderen Umgang mit Texten." *Schreibend(d) lernen. Ideen und Projekte für die Schule.* Ed. Gerd Bräuer. Hamburg: Körber, 2004. 20-26. Print.

Flick, Uwe. *Handbuch qualitative Sozialforschung. Grundlagen, Konzepte,Methoden und Anwendungen.* Weinheim: Beltz Psychologie-Verlag-Union, 1995. Print.

Gläser, Jochen, and Grit Laudel. *Experteninterviews und qualitative Inhaltsanalyse als Instrument rekonstruierender Untersuchungen* Wiesbaden: Verlag für Sozialwissenschaften, 2009. Print.

Harris, Muriel. "Talking in the Middle: Why Writers Need Writing Tutors." *College English* 57.1. (1995): 27-42. Web.

Herkner, L., Mandy Pydde, and Simone Tschirpke. "Paving the Way for Writing Across the Curriculum (WAC): Establishing Writing Centers and Peer Tutoring at High Schools in Germany." *Across the Disciplines* 9.3. (2012). Web. 28 November 2013. <http://wac.colostate.edu/atd/second_educ/herkneretal.cfm>.

Mayring, Phillipp. *Qualitative Inhaltsanalyse: Grundlagen und Techniken.* Weinheim: Deutscher Studien Verlag. 1993. Print.

---. "Qualitative Inhaltsanalyse." *Forum: Qualitative Sozialforschung* 1.2 (2000).

Web. 10 August 2013. <http://www.qualitative-research.net>.
Merz-Grötsch, Jasmin. *Die Wirklichkeit aus Schülersicht. Eine empirische Analyse.* Freiburg: Fillibach, 2001. Print.
Micheel, Christine, and Meike Vogel. "Schreiblabor Bielefeld: Workshops zum wissenschaftlichen Schreiben für Schülerinnen und Schüler." *Schreibend(d) lernen. Ideen und Projekte für die Schule* Ed. Gerd Bräuer. Hamburg: Körber, 2004. 191-207. Print.
Rapp, Rune. "Die Ausbildung von Pädagogikstudenten zu Schreibberatern." *Schreibend(d) lernen. Ideen und Projekte für die Schule.* Ed. Gerd Bräuer. Hamburg: Körber, 2004. 171-81. Print.
Robert Bosch Stiftung. *Robert Bosch Stiftung: Fifty Years Shaping the Future.* n. pag. 2013. Web. 23 June 2013.
Schiller, Erdmuthe. "Online-Bertatung am Schreibzentrum der PH Freiburg." *Schreibend(d) lernen. Ideen und Projekte für die Schule.* Ed. Gerd Bräuer Hamburg: Körber, 2004. 182-90. Print.

CHAPTER 8

"SO MUCH MORE THAN JUST AN 'A'": A TRANSFORMATIVE HIGH SCHOOL AND UNIVERSITY WRITING CENTER PARTNERSHIP

Marie Hansen, Debra Hartley, Kirsten Jamsen, Katie Levin, and Kristen Nichols-Besel

In late 2011, Burnsville High School (BHS) teacher Marie Hansen contacted Kirsten Jamsen, director of the Center for Writing at the University of Minnesota (UMN), with what she thought was a kind of wild request—"Can I bring my high school writing coaches to campus to visit your writing center?" In true Minnesota fashion, Kirsten and the Center's assistant directors Debra Hartley and Katie Levin, along with graduate writing consultant (and former K–12 teacher with an interest in high school writing centers as sites of teacher development) Kristen Nichols-Besel responded, "Ya, you betcha!"—welcoming the opportunity to embark on an experimental and collaborative journey together. The story of this developing partnership between a well-established, multi-location university writing center with a strong focus on writing across the curriculum (WAC) and a small high school writing center located in an English teacher's classroom reveals how curiosity, risk-taking, and grassroots enthusiasm can start and sustain a partnership despite minimal resources.

At the beginning, not one of us had any idea our partnership would go so far, but now, more than two years later, we have created a mutually beneficial program of cross-institutional professional development for both high school student writing coaches and university student writing consultants. Although the success of our partnership is due in large part to our willingness to communicate with each other, jump into action, make mistakes, and be flexible, this is more than a story of individuals. The BHS–UMN partnership grew out of—and continues to enrich—a strong, professional community of educators committed to teaching writing, most notably our mini-regional organization of writing center professionals and the local network of National Writing Project teacher-leaders. In this way our partnership seeks to be what Henry Luce describes as an ideal writing center collaboration: "an on-going and growing community of writers, mutually supportive, mutually instructive" (130).

With our deep and broad engagement in a wide variety of cross-institutional communities of practice, all participants in the partnership saw the collaborative, experimental, inquiry-based values at its core to be a natural part of their writing center work. From the start, we five co-leaders have been energized and sustained by two convictions: (1) student coaches and consultants are capable of—and can learn from each other about—engaging their peers in meaningful conversations about writing across the curriculum, and (2) observing and experiencing the work of another writing center helps us to reflect upon and improve our own practice. We hope this story of our partnership will inspire others to seek out their local networks and take the courageous steps of reaching out across institutional boundaries to find out what others are doing, to ask for help, to share resources, to develop cross-institutional staff education models, or to simply converse as we would in a supportive writing center consultation.

TWO STORYLINES CONVERGE TO FORM A PARTNERSHIP

The initial 2011 connection that kicked off our partnership involved the convergence of two storylines: Marie's individual quest to create the Burnsville High School (BHS) Writing Center in 2008 and Kirsten and Katie's efforts to support the development of high school writing centers in Minnesota, which solidified when they participated in a workshop on high school-university WAC partnerships at a 2010 conference. These stories came together in 2011 during the Minnesota Writing Project Invitational Summer Institute.

In 2008, fresh out of college, Marie began her education career teaching English at BHS, a large public high school in a suburb of Minneapolis. From the beginning she faced frustration. No matter how many times she talked about thesis statements or academic voice in front of the classroom, her students just didn't "get it." Their essays fell short of her expectations, and she could not figure out why she wasn't reaching them. Drawing on her college experience as a writing tutor at Bethel University in St. Paul, Minnesota for two-and-a-half years, she began encouraging her students to come in for after-school conferences before major essays were due.[1] Something wonderful happened when she had one-to-one conversations with her students. Even though she used the exact same words to explain thesis statements, for example, these individual conferences produced the "lightbulb" moments she had been missing in class. She began to see a real change in her students' writing. Despite her sense of success, Marie knew that after-school teacher conferences would not be feasible with 150 students; she couldn't possibly meet with all of them. What if her students could receive writing support similar to what she and her colleagues had given at Bethel?

Marie began researching high school writing centers and found only one in Minnesota: the Minnetonka High School Writing Center (http://www.minnetonka.k12.mn.us/writingcenter), which at that time involved tutoring done by two professional teachers and several parent volunteers.[2] As a first-year teacher, Marie knew she could not ask her administration to pay for something so expensive. But what if she set up a center staffed with peer tutors? As a young teacher, Marie vividly remembered the struggle high school seniors often face as they try to demonstrate community service and extracurricular activities on their college applications. Could she use this need to attract volunteer tutors? She connected with several colleagues who directed the National Honor Society and Youth Service programs at BHS, and they agreed to accept tutoring hours for credit. Motivated by a desire to improve student writing and relying on the competitive nature of college-bound seniors, an idea was born. As Childers, Fels, and Jordan remind us, "All one really needs to start a writing center is an idea of what that writing center will be" (7).

In retrospect, the rest of the process of setting up the BHS Writing Center was simple and refreshingly free of red tape. It involved first talking to departmental colleagues, and then running the idea past the principal in a thirty-second hallway conversation. The principal asked for a brief proposal (¾ page) and meeting (fifteen minutes), after which Marie was officially the proud director of the new BHS Writing Center, opening in fall of 2009.[3] Reflecting back, Marie recognizes that if she had gone into a formal meeting asking for a stipend, money for paying tutors, a paid period to work at the center during the school day, or a fancy space decked out with extra computers and other resources, she would have been turned down. Rather, she took the approach of minimal commitment and maximum student benefit, agreeing that the center would not cost BHS any money, at least not for the first year. After that, she thought, she would be in a better position to ask for resources. Marie also wisely tapped into BHS's strong focus on college readiness for all students, language she heard in every staff meeting and school communication. She had easily sold her administration on the idea of a student-staffed writing center that benefited both high achieving student leaders and struggling students. With invaluable advice about logistics from her friend and former supervisor April Schmidt, director of the Writing Center at Bethel University, Marie recruited tutors for the following school year from the strong writers in her eleventh-grade English classes, put up posters, developed sign-in and record-keeping systems, and organized tutor training.

Even though starting the BHS Writing Center in fall 2009 was easier than she imagined, keeping it stable and helping it to thrive was trickier. By 2011, building and sustaining the BHS Writing Center felt practically impossible to Marie. Drawing on what she remembered from college, Marie and her writing coaches advertised in English classes; begged teachers to send in their students, even if it took bribing them with extra credit; offered to tutor before school, after school, and during tutors' study halls; and simplified every aspect of signing up for a writing consultation. After two years, however, the BHS Writing Center was helping fewer than one hundred students per semester (in a large suburban high school with more than two thousand students), and those clients were almost always coming from Marie's classes. With this writing center functioning more as an extension of Marie's classroom rather than a school-wide opportunity, the coaches were becoming discouraged. Their sessions rarely lasted longer than fifteen minutes, and they began skipping their volunteer shifts.

Enter the Minnesota Writing Project (MWP), the local site of the National Writing Project, housed in the UMN Center for Writing.[4] At UMN, the Center for Writing is a locus of what Robert W. Barnett and Lois M. Rosen call a "campus-wide writing environment" (1): this comprehensive center offers one-to-one writing consultations for students, writing-across-the-curriculum workshops and consultations for instructors, support for research into the ways in which writing can foster learning in and across the disciplines, and a writing-enriched curriculum program that guides academic departments through a process of infusing writing and writing instruction into their undergraduate curricula.[5]

With three years of teaching under her belt, in 2011 Marie was ready for new ideas to improve her teaching and build a professional network beyond her school. Four of Marie's BHS colleagues were teacher consultants through the MWP, and MWP director Muriel Thompson had taught at BHS for many years before retiring and working at UMN. Because of their encouragement and support, Marie participated in the MWP Invitational Summer Institute in June and July of 2011. Here she met teachers from across grade levels and disciplines, and was first introduced to Kirsten and Debra, who help lead the MWP Summer Institute each year. Marie remembers that she had to build up her courage to ask for writing tutor training support from Kirsten and really didn't expect her to say yes.[6]

For Kirsten, saying yes was easy. Even before she and Debra had spent the summer with Marie writing, reading, and participating in teaching demonstrations together during the MWP Summer Institute, Kirsten and many of her colleagues in the Center for Writing had been learning more about high school writing centers, talking with Maggie Shea as she established the Minnetonka High School Writing Center, and thinking about how to support the growth of writing centers in primary and secondary schools in Minnesota. Those thoughts began to take actionable form when Kirsten and Katie participated in Pamela Childers and Jacob Blumner's workshop on High School-University WAC Partnerships at the 2010 International Writing Across the Curriculum conference in

Bloomington, Indiana.

When they were asked to reflect on partnerships in the workshop, Katie and Kirsten recognized how much they had gained from their active participation in professional organizations like the Midwest Writing Centers Association, the International Writing Centers Association, the Conference on College Composition and Communication, and the National Council of Teachers of English. Indeed, at Indiana University that week, they had just participated in a meeting of Big Ten writing center directors and would return home for the next meeting of the Writing Center Professionals of Minnesota (WCPM), an informal mini-regional group of writing and learning center administrators from a wide variety of institutions of higher education across Minnesota. Although WCPM had already proven to be a resource for high school writing centers (with Maggie Shea from Minnetonka High School now attending meetings and, unknown to Katie and Kirsten, WCPM-er April Schmidt supporting Marie's development of the BHS Writing Center), the size of the group (over 100 members) would limit the opportunity for secondary school teachers' voices to be heard. To facilitate a focus on writing centers in secondary and primary schools, the idea for the E12 (Early education through twelfth grade) Writing Centers Collective was born: an informal, grassroots network for anyone leading, starting, or just dreaming about a writing center in a preschool, elementary, or secondary school context.[7] Like WCPM, from which it was an offshoot, the E12 Collective would share the motto "Anyone who comes belongs," encourage information sharing and support among members, and meet regularly at different writing centers. In September 2010, Maggie Shea hosted the first meeting at the Minnetonka High School Writing Center, and since that time this group has met eight times, at six different secondary school writing centers and twice at UMN. Many of the teachers in the E12 Collective are also active MWP teacher consultants, who have helped expand and strengthen the network by inviting colleagues into the group and serving as resources for one another.

Marie's 2011 request for help brought these two separate storylines together and began the process of shaping a collaboration based on shared values, mutual respect, and the desire to create a partnership of benefit to both writing centers. On the surface, the partnership between UMN and BHS may seem improbable. Located at the state's flagship university, the UMN Center for Writing is visible and long-established, drawing on a history of writing tutoring since the early 1970s, of formal programs for writing across the curriculum since 1987, and of National Writing Project site leadership since 1990. Its Student Writing Support (SWS) program has multiple locations, both physical and online; offers computers for student use; provides hundreds of resources and texts; conducts over 10,000 writing consultations each year; and hires undergraduate and graduate students and professionals to work as writing consultants (currently maintaining a staff of forty consultants). At BHS, the writing center is in a corner of Marie's classroom, sign-ups are written on a calendar on the hallway wall outside, student attendance can be inconsistent, and the coaches are high school students. The BHS Writing Center finally secured a computer after four years of existence, but still lacks an internet connection. Despite our vastly different centers, however, we share many of the same beliefs about what writers need and how best to tutor writers, and these shared values allow our partnership to thrive.

A CROSS-INSTITUTIONAL MODEL OF CONSULTANT PROFESSIONAL DEVELOPMENT IS BORN

Shortly after Marie posed her question to Kirsten, we arranged a face-to-face meeting at the UMN Center for Writing to talk about possibilities. Although Marie was meeting Katie and graduate writing consultant Kristen Nichols-Besel (who had been interested in high school writing centers since she first learned about them at the 2008 International Writing Centers Association conference) for the first time, introductions and small talk quickly became action. Kristen volunteered to lead Marie and her BHS coaches on a tour of SWS's two physical locations and demonstrate SWS.online, and together we came up with the idea of having the BHS coaches experience college writing consultations with SWS consultants after SWS closed for the day. This "field trip to the U" would both introduce the BHS coaches to an established university writing center that employs consultants and serves writers from across the disciplines, and give them the experience of sharing their own writing with a writing consultant—something none of them had done before.[8]

The plan became a reality in March 2012, when Marie secured funding from her principal for a bus and brought fifteen coaches to campus for a five-hour visit, which also included lunch at the student union with former BHS coaches who were now UMN students, and a chance to tour campus before meeting with Kristen. As the BHS coaches watched college students meeting face-to-face with SWS consultants in two locations and saw a brief presentation about SWS. online consultations, Kristen and Marie encouraged these high school seniors to use and consider applying for work at the writing centers of the colleges they would attend the following year. Then, the doors of SWS were closed to UMN students, and the cross-institutional activity began.

We formed groups of three—one SWS consultant and two BHS writing coaches—for two rounds of thirty-minute consultations. The BHS students brought their own writing, including personal essays for college applications that had already been submitted, and essays for their challenging College in the

Schools writing and economics courses. While each SWS consultant worked with a BHS coach on her/his writing, the other coach observed and took notes, using a set of guiding questions (see Appendix 1). Then, the consultee and observer switched roles and rotated to work with a different SWS consultant for a second round of thirty-minute consultations and observations. Finally, we all met in a forty-minute, large-group debriefing discussion, sharing what coaches experienced as consultees and recorded while observing, and using the debriefing questions to focus our discussion. The BHS coaches were eager to talk during the debrief, noting that they were surprised by how much the SWS consultants negotiated agenda-setting with them and put them in the role of expert on the content of their writing. Many of the BHS coaches were enthusiastic about the experience of interacting with the SWS consultants, who were interested in and respectful of their ideas, as well as encouraging about ways the writers could improve and revise their papers. As Kevin (a pseudonym) noted, this interaction with a consultant made him realize how talking about how to improve a paper and grow as a writer was about "so much more than just an 'A.'" Similarly, the SWS consultants shared how much they enjoyed working with writers who brought strong, polished drafts and were motivated to be there and learn more about expectations for college-level writing.

Upon returning to BHS, Marie noticed a powerful change in how her coaches worked with writers. Before, their sessions were very short, averaging just fifteen minutes. Indeed, in her initial training, she had put so much emphasis on prioritizing global over local concerns (in other words, tackling thesis and organization before grammar and word choice) that her coaches seemed to think that the only way they could cover all those issues in a session was to rush through their suggestions quickly. After working with SWS consultants, her coaches began conducting thirty-minute consultations using the specific strategies employed by the SWS consultants, such as reading an essay slowly out loud or mirroring back what they heard in the student's draft ("What I hear you saying is ... Is that correct?"). Instead of telling student writers what to do to get a better grade, they began asking questions that could encourage writers to take ownership over their papers and draw out their own ideas for revision: "What is the purpose of this paragraph?" "How do you think this idea fits in with your thesis?" and "How did you realize this claim was true when you were reading the book?" From working with the SWS consultants, the BHS coaches realized that their role was not to tell the students what was wrong with their essays and send them out the door; rather, they could ask students about their own goals and purposes, encourage them to help guide the session, and use questions and conversation to facilitate the student writers' own thinking and writing. As they developed these skills, the BHS coaches realized that they did not need to have taken a class to help a student writing for that class; instead, they could, like SWS consultants, rely on the student writers for content expertise, no matter what the discipline.

With such marked improvement in the work of her coaches (all of whom graduated in June 2012), Marie was eager to bring her next cohort of coaches to UMN sooner, when they were first learning how to consult. In October 2012, Marie brought nineteen new BHS coaches, and we followed the same field trip schedule and three-person consultation and debrief protocol.[9] These new coaches were very engaged in their consultations, but during the debriefing were more reluctant to share their impressions of what happened; in retrospect, this reluctance was not surprising, because most had not yet seen any student clients in their center and were therefore at a loss when we asked them to draw comparisons between the two centers. Nonetheless, Marie noticed again that her coaches began to mimic the strategies they observed as they began consulting in their center. Because the BHS coaches were so engaged in their SWS consultations, they returned to BHS with high expectations for engagement in consultations with their fellow BHS students. We learned later that they were disappointed when BHS student writers requested quick corrections rather than engaging in more substantive conversations about their work and their process.

To give SWS consultants a chance to hear about what the coaches had been doing since their visit and to challenge the hierarchy we had created of high school coaches learning how to tutor from university consultants, a small number of the SWS consultants who participated in the October collaboration visited the BHS Writing Center in May 2013. We hoped this role reversal would help the BHS coaches gain confidence in their ability to help experienced writers with unfamiliar assignments and begin to see themselves as part of and contributing to a larger writing center community. During the first part of the visit, the BHS coaches explained how their sessions had worked during the year and described sessions that they enjoyed or struggled with—noting that they enjoyed sessions where the writer had ideas to discuss, but they disliked the sessions in which it was difficult to get the writer to talk. The BHS coaches (all seniors) also admitted that they were often most comfortable working with papers from classes they had taken and assignments they were familiar with, leading to a discussion about working with students writing in different subject areas, expertise, authority, and the triangulated relationship between tutors, teachers, and students. When the seven SWS consultants shared their writing with the Burnsville coaches, we connected each university writer with at least two BHS coaches. Many of the coaches seemed uncomfortable giving feedback on the university consultants' writing, although they were very eager to find out more about the expectations of college-level writing and talk about their own college plans—not surprising for graduating seniors. After the visit, some shared with Marie that they felt a significant barrier between themselves and "expert" university-level consultants, something the next phase of our partnership will try to address more explicitly.

Despite the complexities of coordinating field trips between our centers, we all agree that this partnership has been a positive and affirming experience. Both writing centers believe in the value of peer tutoring, a minimum of hierarchy, and respect for all writers. Although many high schools use college students, pre-service teachers, parent volunteers, or their own school staff as writing consultants, Marie has always believed in her students' capabilities to ask thoughtful, probing questions and engage in intelligent conversations with their peers. UMN's writing consultants affirmed her faith in the competency of the BHS coaches. During these practice consultations and discussions, the SWS consultants and high school coaches developed camaraderie and a mutual respect. Their interactions also demonstrated the power of conversation between a careful questioner/listener and a writer in an unfamiliar course or discipline. With guidance from experienced consultants at UMN, BHS coaches are gaining confidence and developing their tutoring repertoire.

Similarly, the directors of both centers appreciate the benefits of flexibility. Rather than becoming stonewalled by bureaucracy and red tape, we all believe in finding a way to work around restrictions. When confronted with low funding, for example, we are all willing to find creative solutions. Marie has been leading her writing center as extra service without a stipend, her student coaches work without pay, and her principal funds her bus for field trips to UMN out of a special account. UMN consultants participate in these collaborations as part of their paid professional development time. UMN consultants pay for their own travel to Burnsville when we meet there. Maintaining this flexible and generous attitude, rather than assuming that things must work a certain way, has allowed us to accomplish much more together.[10]

In addition to providing valuable professional development for coaches and consultants in both centers, this partnership has had a positive effect on the growth of E12 writing centers in our area. One of the most powerful moments in the partnership was when in May 2012, a few months after our first collaboration, Marie and her coaches hosted a meeting of the E12 Writing Centers Collective. In this meeting, attended by teachers involved in teacher- and parent-led writing centers in their schools as well as those getting ready to launch new centers, a panel of Marie's coaches reflected on the experience of coming to UMN two months earlier, shared how and why they volunteer their time in the center, and responded to many questions about what they would recommend for establishing writing centers and supporting peer coaches. The teachers in the E12 Collective still talk about how impressed they were by Marie's coaches, and the writing center directors at both a large public urban high school and small private suburban school later shared how much that conversation influenced their own thinking about what their centers could be.

As we hope our story reveals, the values of this cross-institutional writing center partnership are also WAC values. In making a case for the natural connection between WAC and writing centers, Steven Corbett and Michelle LaFrance articulate the shared WAC/writing center beliefs that "students come to understand writing conventions as the products of disciplinary communities when they can compare writing tasks and conventions across disciplinary contexts"; that "writers at all levels of proficiency benefit from thinking about the often unspoken assumptions of 'effective' writing within particular contexts"; and that "the writing center [is] a *cross-curricular way of learning*" (2, 6). We believe that our collaboration is, to paraphrase Corbett and LaFrance, a *cross-institutional way of learning*. The same kinds of conversation, listening, collaborative problem-solving, and co-learning across disciplines that take place in a WAC writing center undergird many of our shared professional networks and are at the heart of our BHS–UMN partnership. We are excited that our partnership has begun to encourage and nurture other cross-institutional collaborations, as we've shared our learning-in-progress with members of Writing Center Professionals of Minnesota and the E12 Writing Centers Collective.

From our partnership, we have seen evidence of many dimensions of cross-institutional learning—for all parties involved.

1. The high school coaches developed a collaborative, conversational philosophy of tutoring, which made them more confident in their ability to help others, and gave them specific consulting approaches to enact this philosophy.

The story of one BHS writing coach reveals the powerful effect of participating in university writing consultations. Marie was nervous at the beginning of the year because one of her coaches, Callie (a pseudonym), was extremely shy. Callie panicked every time she had to speak in public and told Marie she felt uncomfortable telling students how to write an essay. Conscientious and thoughtful, Callie was afraid she would offend writers with blunt directions, creating a big challenge for her as a coach. Callie did not speak much during her visit to UMN, but Marie noticed her approach to tutoring immediately changed after that visit. Callie became one of Marie's most successful coaches because she asked so many thoughtful questions. Marie believes that Callie realized by participating in and observing conferences in SWS that she didn't need to tell students what to do or have the "right" answers; she just needed to have a conversation. Callie felt confident initiating a conversation because it didn't require as much directiveness as she first assumed, and she found herself able to help her peers much more. As they become comfortable with asking questions and drawing out student knowledge in the consultations, BHS coaches are better prepared to work with students writing across the disciplines.

After both visits to UMN, Marie noticed all of her consultants trying the very strategies they observed SWS consultants using with them: asking writers to share their goals and concerns, negotiating an agenda together, asking probing questions, mirroring back what they heard in a text, encouraging a writer's ownership and self-assessment of their writing, and talking about one's writing process beyond the text in front of them. Even the English teachers at BHS took notice, commenting to Marie about the coaches' use of questioning and conversation in the writing center and during in-class peer review sessions. BHS student clients have also noted that the coaches ask the same kinds of questions their teachers do.

2. As the BHS Writing Center began using a collaborative, conversational approach that talked about writing as more than just "English papers," both consultants and student writers began to consider how this work involves negotiations around disciplinary knowledge, previous writing experiences, and levels of expertise and authority.

During their visits, BHS coaches observed and worked with both undergraduate and graduate SWS consultants from a wide range of majors, such as American studies, biology, education, history, political science, and theatre. The fact that SWS consultants shared their perspectives on writing in different fields and at different levels—and did not know anything about the BHS English teachers who encourage much of the BHS Writing Center activity—opened up the high school coaches to talking about writing across the curriculum and for different audiences and purposes.

In fact, it was the BHS writing coaches and students in her class who alerted Marie to the buzz around school about a particularly challenging historiography assignment, opening the door for the writing center to work more closely with AP United States History teachers and their students. When Marie emailed the history teachers to chat, they were open to sharing what they were looking for in these essays—sending her their rubric, a checklist of important things to remember, and a relevant PowerPoint presentation.[11] Although only a small number of students are using the writing center for their historiography essays so far, Marie and the history teachers are eager to continue working together in future semesters by publicizing their partnership to students early in the process.

This expanded view of writing also encouraged student clients to see the value in a conversation between peers and that they too could become writing coaches. For example, when honors student Keisha (a pseudonym) began visiting the BHS Writing Center several times without receiving extra credit as most students did, Marie became curious and pulled her aside after class to ask if she was struggling with the assignment or had any questions. Keisha explained that it helped to talk about her ideas with someone else while she was writing her college application essays. Despite her anxiety with this high-stakes writing, when Keisha went home each night with a new question from her coach to answer, she was able to write a little bit more, return the next day for more help, and repeat the process. Keisha's continued writing center usage would never have happened if her coach, Austin (a pseudonym), who both visited UMN in October 2012 and participated in the May 2013 discussion at BHS, had not focused on asking so many questions about Keisha's experiences, probing her for more information about what she had learned. Austin's approach to these meetings as an informal conversation between two writers chatting about ideas and word choice significantly reduced Keisha's stress. Her final essay was excellent, and she applied to be a coach for 2013–14, largely because of this experience.

3. High school writing coaches and their student clients gained support in preparing for college, while, at the same time, university writing consultants gained valuable insight into the high school-to-college transition from working with high school writers.

The initial connection between the BHS Writing Center and college readiness appealed to the BHS administration, in part because of the center's contribution to what Luce identifies as "bridging the gap between high school and college ... ensuring the continuity of excellence throughout the system" (129). Similarly, in their survey of secondary school and university WAC partnerships, Blumner and Childers note the common desire of high schools to "create seamless transitions between high school and college" (92). Students who visit the BHS Writing Center benefit from learning that asking for help is okay, and have become more aware of writing centers and other academic support resources in college. Senior coaches appreciate the opportunity to *be in college* during their field trips, are eager to share what they experienced with their peers, and begin to see opportunities for student leadership that they can take advantage of when they leave high school in just one year.

For example, at the first UMN field trip, BHS senior Allie Waters connected with Kristen about the University of Northern Iowa (UNI), which Kristen had attended as an undergraduate and which Allie planned to attend in the fall. Once at UNI, Allie started visiting the writing center with her own essays, and then she was hired as a tutor at the end of her freshman year. She tells us no one at UNI can figure out how an accounting major ended up becoming a writing center tutor and even publishing a short story in the campus literary magazine. Allie acknowledges that she probably wouldn't have considered the possibility without having the background as a high school writing coach and visiting the UMN Center for Writing. In addition, several graduated BHS coaches have told Marie how quickly they began using their university writing centers, and we are eager for those attending UMN to apply to be undergraduate writing consultants. Clearly, college students are more likely to visit a center if they have already observed its value, rather than entering college believing there is a stigma associated with asking for help with writing.

We have also learned that the word "college" bears so much weight for high schoolers because they see it as a place where people are intelligent, capable, and have the "right" answers. When they worked with the UMN consultants on campus, the BHS coaches were very receptive to the consultants' ideas because they arrived ready to learn. In addition, when Marie and her graduating coaches passed out applications for next year's coaches, only a few students were interested. After Marie reminded the coaches, "Tell them about the U!" and her coaches described the training at UMN, many more hands went up. These prospective coaches believe that they will be effective writing coaches next year, not because they see themselves as strong writers, but because they assume working with consultants at the UMN can get them there, as both writers and coaches.

Building off this strong interest in college readiness, the BHS Writing Center has marketed itself as the place to prepare for college, offering a semi-annual "Grammar Crammer" before the eleventh grade grammar final exam each semester. In this popular event, which attracted over 100 students in 2012–13, BHS Writing Center coaches help students correct extra practice questions, which are similar to those in the high-stakes ACT verbal section. Similarly, the BHS Writing Center sponsors a panel of local college admissions directors who share their insights into college application essays, and then follows that panel with a week of additional tutoring hours to help application essay writers.

As the BHS coaches asked about college more generally during their consultations, the UMN writing consultants found themselves in the role of guides and insiders. Many consultants enjoyed sharing stories about their own transitions from high school to college and their suggestions for making the most out of college and being successful as a student. For the youngest and newest UMN undergraduate consultants, this partnership provided a rare opportunity for them to feel a sense of expertise among their more experienced colleagues, many of whom are graduate students and professionals.

The UMN consultants also expanded their understanding of the transition from high school to college-level writing and how they can best help first-year students—affirming Cox and Gimbel's argument, in Chapter 2 of this book, that those in high schools and colleges have much to learn from each other about how writing is used in each other's context. Though many consultants commented that working with these high school seniors was similar in many ways to working with college freshmen, they were able to have conversations with the students about high school writing and the students' concerns about the upcoming transition from high school to college. They appreciated the opportunity to expand their understanding of this transition and to talk with highly motivated high school writers about their strong, very polished drafts.

4. Directors at both the high school and university writing centers found support, connection, and inspiration through this partnership, which became a touchstone for their larger community of writing center professionals.

The learning arising from this partnership was not limited to coaches and consultants, as the directors of both centers gained significantly from the project. During her first two years running the BHS Writing Center, Marie felt a bit like she was living on a deserted island. If she had not met the Center for Writing staff in 2011, she questions whether she would have continued the BHS Writing Center. She likely would have become discouraged and run out of new ideas to try to bring students in, as both coaches and clients. Buoyed by the positive energy of this partnership and the enthusiasm her coaches have for our collaboration, Marie has greater confidence and belief in the value of her efforts. Not surprisingly, her center has become more visible, her student usage has tripled, and more students apply to be coaches each year.

Kirsten, Debra, and Katie have long been supportive of local secondary writing centers through hosting meetings of the E12 Writing Centers Collective and meeting individually with secondary teachers starting their own centers. Yet those conversations have often felt one-way, sharing UMN practices without deep knowledge of what is really possible in a high school writing center. The collaborative nature of the BHS-UMN partnership opened our eyes to the realities of writing consultancy in a high school setting: where and when it happens, the kinds of assignments and audiences high school writers face, and—most importantly— who the high school coaches are and what motivates them as writers and consultants. The fact we have pulled off regular field trips and meetings has strengthened and inspired the larger E12 Writing Centers Collective as well, building our grassroots network to be one where we visit each others' centers and share our practices together.

5. University directors were able to use the partnership as a key component of their staff professional development efforts, providing them and their consultants a fresh perspective on their own practice, questioning their assump-

tions, seeing alternatives, and wrestling with challenging questions raised by our different writing center contexts.

As the lively full-group discussion in our March 2012 meeting revealed, all participants were intrigued by the differences between our writing center contexts and how our pedagogies adapt to and push against those contexts. Faced with curious young coaches who wanted to learn how to tutor, university consultants had the opportunity to articulate the strategies and beliefs behind their practices. Although the UMN Center for Writing consultants participate in professional development on a regular basis, rarely do the consultants have the chance to have such in-depth conversations about their practices with eager learners who are curious and appreciative. As UMN undergraduate consultant Damian Johansson describes:

> I love working with the Burnsville tutors. It is always exciting to work with people that are purely interested in the topic of work, and these kids were so ready to talk and learn about tutoring, making for a fun, informative, and truly productive day. I would have described it as relaxed, but the sessions were so charged with interested participants that it wasn't exactly relaxed, but still enjoyable.
>
> During spring semester last year we visited the tutors at the Burnsville campus, bringing our work for their consideration. I decided to push this unique experience further by bringing a creative piece with me for consultation. The tutor I worked with was both flabbergasted and excited to review a creative piece. He was a creative writer himself, and although slightly daunted, he volunteered to work with me. We talked about creative writing in general, and after he confided his love of creative writing to me, I asked if he had any of his writing with him. As all writers should, he had hardcopy with him. I asked if, while he read my piece, I could read some of his. This broke down the barrier of perceived authority/old dudeness that he was shackled with, and he dove into his backpack. We read, side by side, both making noises of enjoyment or interest as we read. Afterwards, we first talked about my piece, as this was my session for help, and then I generally talked about my perceptions of his piece, mostly responding to his direct questions about it.

Not only did the university and high school tutors make connections and develop a sense of "peerness," as Damian describes, but the experience of stepping into another writing center helped them explore such controversial issues as consultant expertise and the triangulated relationship between consultants, teachers, and students. As UMN undergraduate writing consultant Alysha Bohanon reflected recently:

> Even if you've taken the same class as the student [at UMN], the chance of you taking that class with the same professor is slim. High school is very different, and I wonder how these coaches would go about separating their personal experience in a class from their position as a tutor. Shielding your expertise wouldn't work when the student already knows you had to have taken the class, since you are in the same school. It was especially interesting to me that one of the reasons Burnsville teachers referred students to the writing center was because the coaches had already taken the class and knew what was expected in the assignment—I'm not sure how the high school coaches could possibly escape their expertise in this scenario.
>
> Despite the different atmospheres of high school and college writing, I think a version of this pressure to "make it do what the professor wants" creeps into our center sometimes, particularly with undergraduate writers. It's still so much about grades and pleasing your professor at that level, even if there is more creativity involved. I've seen too many written comments from professors telling students to come to the center to figure out what is expected in an assignment, as though we are not only experts in every discipline, but also mind readers for confusing assignment sheets.

Seeing the constraints of the high school writing center made visible to UMN consultants the often invisible constraints in our university context, opening us all up to deeper conversations about working with writers across the curriculum and negotiating expertise that have continued in our ongoing staff development.

LOOKING TO THE FUTURE

The UMN consultants who have participated in the consultations and conversations with BHS coaches are helping to keep our collaboration going by regularly asking, "When are we going to see the high schoolers again?" and "How's the Burnsville High School Writing Center doing?" As we move into our third year of the partnership, once-per-semester BHS visits have begun to feel like another regular form of staff development in the Center for Writing, alongside regularly scheduled Friday staff meetings and discussions.

Drawing on the flexibility and risk-taking that marked the start of our partnership, we continue to experiment with new strategies for our centers and our collaboration. For example, Marie has begun to call her tutors "coaches," rather than tutors. Although writing center literature has used the "coach" metaphor since as early as 1986 (see, for example, Muriel Harris's *Teaching One-to-One*), this particular decision stems from a conversation during the May 2013 UMN visit to BHS, where we talked together about the parallels between athletic coaching and coaching writers. We believe that for high-schoolers, who are often familiar with a coaching philosophy from their experiences with youth athletics, this name change may promote a new style of tutoring, as well as confidence. In addition, as part of their staff development, Marie's coaches are now reading excerpts from Dawn Fels and Jennifer Wells's *The Successful High School Writing Center* (including Alexandra Elchinoff and Caroline Kowalski's chapter, "The Tutors Speak," to bring in perspectives from yet another school). They will also write a literacy narrative essay, the same one that new UMN undergraduate writing consultants write in Kirsten's Theory and Practice of Writing Consultancy class, before visiting UMN (Appendix 2). We hope this shared assignment will create more of a common ground between the high school coaches and UMN writing consultants who have written it themselves in Kirsten's class or are familiar with this annual assignment. We hope that by responding to the assignment prompts about personal reading and writing history, BHS coaches may realize that they all have the background necessary to contribute to a conversation about literacy.

In future years, Marie will hire new coaches sooner than the last few weeks of school, creating more continuity from year to year in our partnership. During April, there is usually a lull in the BHS center, and senior coaches begin to lose focus at the end of the year. Marie plans to sign up new junior coaches and organize training sessions throughout the spring with both incoming and experienced coaches, including the spring visit from UMN tutors. Therefore, three types of tutors will be able to participate in mock consultations and observations—SWS consultants, BHS senior coaches, and BHS junior prospective coaches—fostering a feeling of expertise and continued commitment from both incoming and experienced coaches.

Recognizing that the heart of our collaboration is the interaction happening between the high school coaches and university consultants, we will continue to work on breaking down the barriers to open sharing and discussion, experimenting with small group discussions to debrief the practice consultations before moving to large group conversations. Inspired by the work of Rebecca L. Damon and Melody Denny at the Oklahoma State University Writing Center and Writing Project, we are considering using a structured, shared blog, where SWS consultants and BHS coaches can talk about their experiences and offer each other support.

The success of our partnership has also helped generate enthusiasm across our E12 Writing Centers Collective for more cross-institutional learning among our growing number of secondary writing centers. At the last E12 meeting, Marie and Kelly Langdon, who directs the Farmington High School Writing Center, began talking about an August mini-conference for student coaches, which would help meet the training needs of novice coaches, provide a valuable form of leadership and professional development for experienced coaches, and expand our network to include more student voices and ideas.

Those student voices are essential for the BHS Writing Center to be seen as a resource for students and teachers across the curriculum. Marie continues to ask her coaches and students in her classes to tell her about their challenging essays in other courses so she can reach out to the teachers, and so that the writing center can set up help sessions, much like the after-school and evening "writing parties" around common assignments that take place in the Minnetonka High School Writing Center. Based on the positive interest she has already received from the advanced placement U.S. History teachers, Marie sees much potential in explicit WAC outreach to social studies and AVID (Advancement Via Individual Determination) teachers.

After more than four years since the BHS Writing Center's beginning and two years into our partnership, we are all proud that the BHS Writing Center has become a more visible and ingrained part of school culture. BHS students and teachers know what the center is, and Marie's coaches hosted approximately three hundred separate student visits during 2012–13 in various formats. BHS English teachers have committed to encouraging students to come in after school, sometimes by offering extra credit and other incentives and setting up sessions where coaches visit their classes. In addition, many of the new coaches for 2013–2014 have used the center multiple times as sophomore and junior students. In fact, several of them have taken a college preparatory class for capable students who need a bit of extra guidance to reach college readiness, which includes a requirement to visit the BHS Writing Center once a semester. These future coaches already understand the value of a thoughtful conversation about their essays, so we are excited to see how they challenge the past divide between BHS Writing Center coaches (typically honors students who had not used the center) and clients (typically underclassmen needing extra help). With increased visibility and a growing understanding among coaches of the value of one-to-one consultations for *all* writers, the BHS Writing Center has the potential to be seen as a resource for students and teachers at all levels and across the curriculum.

Looking to the future, we are striving for small increments of growth in our partnership over time, and we are patient enough to develop cross-curricular models that fit our local context. We will continue to incorporate all three of the basic components of collaboration described by Blumner and Childers in their study of successful university-secondary school WAC partnerships: we will engage in "information exchange," "involve students," and continue to "provide support" through human and financial resources (95-97). With the UMN partnership, BHS coaches are more effectively trained and feel more confident working with students' writing across the curriculum, and Marie no longer feels as if she is alone on an island. Conversations with Kirsten, Katie, Debra, and Kristen have inspired Marie more than any other resource, and the feeling of mutual benefit for all members of the partnership—and our surrounding networks—is palpable. Marie will share her story and start-up strategies at the Minnesota Council of Teachers of English Conference in April 2014—with, not surprisingly, her coaches presenting alongside her.

NOTES

1. It is such positive past experiences with writing centers that Trixie Smith identifies in Chapter 10 as motivators of successful high school-college collaborations.

2. For more information about the Minnetonka High School Writing Center, see Childers and Lowry. Minnetonka now has a large staff of volunteer student coaches in addition to teachers and parents and is actively involved in supporting teachers using writing across the curriculum.

3. This teacher-driven process contrasts with McMullen's experience, described in Chapter 6, in which the academic dean decided his school needed a writing center.

4. See http://www.nwp.org/cs/public/print/resource_topic/writing_centers for evidence of the many ways NWP supports secondary school writing centers.

5. See http://writing.umn.edu.

6. This experience is an illustration of Trixie Smith's point in Chapter 10 that collaborations often originate through personal connections.

7. See http://writing.umn.edu/sws/e12wcc/index.html.

8. For another model of shared professional development among high school and college writing consultants, see Henry Luce's description of the collaboration between Red Bank Regional High School and Monmouth College (134).

9. See our video about this visit at http://mediamill.cla.umn.edu/mediamill/display/174825.

10. In Chapter 10, Trixie Smith describes many other ways that writing centers can interact with schools and community organizations that do not require a lot of time and money.

11. This openness from content area teachers in response to Marie's outreach is a step towards the kinds of "faculty risk taking" Pamela Childers describes in her collaborations with science and math teachers at McCallie School in "Writing Center or Experimental Center for Faculty Research, Discovery, and Risk Taking?"

WORKS CITED

Barnett, Robert W., and Lois M. Rosen. "The WAC/Writing Center Partnership: Creating a Campus-wide Writing Environment." *Writing Centers and Writing Across the Curriculum Programs: Building Interdisciplinary Partnerships.* Eds. Robert W. Barnett and Jacob S. Blumner. Westport: Greenwood P, 1999. 1-12. Print.

Blumner, Jacob and Pamela Childers: "Building Better Bridges: What Makes High School-College WAC Collaborations Work?" *WAC Journal* 22 (2011): 91-101. Web.

Childers, Pamela B. "Writing Center or Experimental Center for Faculty Research, Discovery, and Risk Taking?" *Writing Centers and Writing Across the Curriculum Programs: Building Interdisciplinary Partnerships.* Eds. Robert W. Barnett and Jacob S. Blumner. Westport: Greenwood P, 1999. 178-86. Print.

Childers, Pamela B., Dawn Fels, and Jeannette Jordan. "The Secondary School Writing Center: A Place to Build Confident, Competent Writers." *Praxis: A Writing Center Journal* 2.1 (2001): n. pag. Web. 26 July 2008.

Childers, Pamela B., and Michael J. Lowry. "Introduction to Writing Across the Curriculum in Secondary Schools." *Across the Disciplines* 9.3 (8 Dec 2012): n. pag. Web. 25 July 2013.

Corbett, Steven, and Michelle LaFrance. "From Grammatical to Global: The WAC/Writing Center Connection." *Praxis: A Writing Center Journal* 6.2 (2009): n. pag. Web. 6 June 2013.

Damron, Rebecca L., and Melody Denny. "Creating Community Partnerships Through Peer Tutoring." Presentation at *IWCA Collaborative @ CCCC 2012, St. Louis, 21 March 2012.*

Fels, Dawn, and Jennifer Wells. *The Successful High School Writing Center.* New York: Teachers College P, 2011. Print.

Harris, Muriel. *Teaching One-to-One: The Writing Conference.* Urbana, IL:

NCTE, 1986. Print.

Luce, Henry A. "High School–College Collaboration." *The High School Writing Center: Establishing and Maintaining One*. Ed. Pamela Childers. WAC Clearinghouse Landmark Publications in Writing Studies: <http://wac.colostate.edu/books/hswc/>. Web. 1 Aug 2013. [Originally Published in Print, 1989, by Urbana: National Council of Teachers of English, Urbana. 1989. 127–35.]

Appendix 1: Handout used during visits to the U of MN's Center for Writing

Consulting Across the High School—College Transition:
Burnsville High School Writing Coaches meet University of Minnesota Writing Consultants
Friday 9 March 2012, 2:15-4:15pm, 15 Nicholson Hall
When you are observing a consultation, please take some notes on the following:
What did you notice?
Who held the pen/pencil/typed on the keyboard?
Where was the paper?
How would you characterize the nonverbal communication?
How would you characterize the talk in the consultation?
What surprised you?
What might you try doing in your own coaching from watching the consultant?

During our debrief after the consultations, we'll discuss the above questions as well as the following:
How did it feel when you were the student writer?
What did the writing consultants do to make writers feel comfortable? Engaged? Motivated to write/revise?
What did the coaches learn about college writing from the consultations?
What did the consultants learn about working with CIS students from the consultations?
How do the consultations at Burnsville compare to the consultations we did today (length of time, type of conversations, etc.)?
What roles do we play as consultants?

Appendix 2: Assignment used in Jamsen's Theory and Practice of Writing Consultancy course at the university each fall; BHS writing coaches will draft their own literacy autobiographies as part of their

fall 2013 training and bring them for consultations at the university

Literacy Autobiography

Draft Due: Tue 18 Sept
Bring two copies of your complete draft (must have a beginning, a middle, and an end) this day for our in-class consultations

Final Version Due: Thur 27 Sept
As with all three of major papers in this course, you will submit the final version as a portfolio, which is the culmination of your entire process of developing, writing, sharing, and revising this paper. Even if you tend to do most of your revision work on the computer, be sure to print out the various notes, outlines, and versions to show me evidence of that process. And, as you revise, please attend to the grading criteria for this assignment listed below.

Length: 3-5 pages

Genre: The literacy autobiography is both personal and analytical. This assignment asks you to reflect upon and analyze your own experiences learning to read and write, ultimately focusing around a central idea about your literacy development that you want to share with our classroom community.

As you saw in the model papers, a successful autobiography must be focused, vivid and descriptive. As readers, we want to see, hear, and feel your experience. But, this assignment also asks you to analyze your experiences. You will make crucial decisions about what experiences to discuss and how to connect those key experiences into a central argument about your own development as a literate person or about your attitude towards your literacy. After reading your autobiography, we should come away with an understanding of both what you experienced and how and why those experiences were significant in your development.

I encourage you to approach this essay creatively, giving yourself plenty of time to reflect and brainstorm before attempting to bring your argument together. Here are several questions to help you get started. You definitely won't want to tackle all of them in a 3-5 page paper, so once you've brainstormed fully, you'll want to narrow and focus your paper. As you think about your experiences, you may also find an angle that is different than any I've suggested here.

Brainstorming questions:

Looking around your home, your backpack, your vehicle, etc., what are the artifacts of your literacy practices? (consider not just the obvious things like books and newspapers, but also the little things like scraps of paper, Post-Its, visual texts, etc.)

What were the artifacts of literacy in your childhood?

When and how did you first learn to read? To write?

What were your parents' or other family members' attitudes about literacy?

What was your experience of reading and writing in school? Was it different than outside of school?

Were there any specific moments when your attitude towards reading/writing changed?

Were there any times when you were challenged to read and write in a new discourse (say, for your major or for a job)?

What was (and is) pleasurable about reading/writing? What was (and is) challenging?

How do you see yourself as a reader/writer now?

Are there ways that your own literacy helps or hinders you?

Grading Criteria:

Process

1. Evidence of significant drafting and revising processes.
2. Awareness of audience and reader feedback.

Focus, Evidence, and Analysis

3. Focus on an appropriate story/argument about your own literacy.
4. Development of a compelling personal narrative with vivid details as evidence ("showing").
5. Rigorous analysis of personal experience, drawing logical conclusions ("telling").

Product

6. Clear, coherent, engaging style.
7. Professional presentation (format, technical details, attention to correctness at the sentence level).

CHAPTER 9

"OH, I GET BY WITH A LITTLE HELP FROM MY FRIENDS": SHORT-TERM WRITING CENTER/ COMMUNITY COLLABORATIONS

Trixie G. Smith

Throughout this collection you have read about long-term WAC partnerships between universities, community colleges, high schools, and other institutions that have been successful over many years, and others that have been learning moments for those involved. When I first became a writing center director, these kinds of long-term partnerships sounded exciting, but they also felt a bit overwhelming and possibly even impossible to achieve with *my* present writing center and resources. What I found, however, was that I could start small and build (see Chapters 2 and 8 for examples of such progressions). Over the years, I have come to value the affordances and returns of short-term collaborations between my WAC-based university writing center and local schools and community groups, as well as more distant partners who can collaborate electronically. All of these collaborations have shown that sometimes partners just need a jumpstart, a little help in conceiving of and planning for the possibilities, to get started with new programming. It doesn't mean that the university or our writing center isn't willing to partner on a more long-term basis; in fact, knowing that we're in the background and willing to help may be the best support for new programs and their participants. Connecting local schools to state and regional writing networks can be ideal, giving them a variety of partnership choices and opportunities. Short-term partnerships also have the advantage of low costs, small upfront commitments (which may be an advantage to a public school or non-profit with an uncertain future), and fewer logistical problems. Despite these low-stakes investments, the payoff can be rich and rewarding for area teachers, students, and community members, as well as the writing center, the WAC program, writing center and WAC staff, and the university.

In this chapter, therefore, I'd like to briefly outline why short-term partnerships are worth your time and energy (and perhaps, your money), then give some examples of various short-term WAC partnerships that have occurred in or through our writing center, which also serves as our de facto writing across and in the disciplines program. Then I would like to close with a case study of a program at our institution, Grandparents University—a program that illustrates how short-term collaborations can not only be rewarding on their own, but can also grow into larger more long-term partnerships—and a set of recommendations for building your own short-term partnerships.

WHY SHORT-TERM PARTNERSHIPS

Schools, community groups, and individuals all seek collaborations for a variety of different reasons. Their motivations may come from within their own programs or schools, or may grow from outside pressures and expectations. Some of the reasons I've encountered include the following:

1. Lack of knowledge or experience: The English teacher asked to start a writing center when she has no writing center experience. The committee asked to plan a writing-across-the-curriculum program for its school. The non-profit director with volunteers asking for additional training.
2. The ever-increasing strains of federal and state testing and the consequent drive to "improve writing."
3. Grant demands to develop partnerships.
4. Teacher or program desires to write in new and different ways.
5. Requests from community members, patrons, students, or parents.
6. Past positive experiences with writing centers, as students perhaps or even as former consultants (often with (y)our writing center specifically).
7. Personal connections with the center, director, or staff of a writing or WAC program.

The motivations of potential partners may not directly match our own objectives, but in my experience, as long as potential partners have complementary goals, the collaborations can be beneficial for both parties—for the day, the week, or the year.

At most colleges and universities, there are a number of different vision and goal statements that blanket the work that we do; you can usually turn to these statements when seeking justification for investments with partners, whether it be for the time you and your staff will donate to the project or the materials, space, or finances needed to make the project successful. At Michigan State University, for example, there are at least three different goal statements that call for investment in the community, for giving students hands-on experiences in the world, and for developing and supporting research: our Boldness By Design campaign (http://boldnessbydesign.msu.edu/), the more recent Bolder By

Design campaign, which adds to the original plan (http://bolderbydesign.msu.edu/), and our Liberal Learning Goals (http://learninggoals.undergrad.msu.edu/goals). In addition, the writing center has its own articulation of these university goals and its own mission guiding the work of the center. As these various statements and goals overlap, four particular goals have risen to the surface for guiding the work in our writing center:

1. The call from our president to move from a land-grant to a world-grant university;
2. The mission of both our university and our writing center to serve the greater community;
3. The culture of family and long-term commitment we strive to develop with our writing center staff and across the university as a whole (Spartans for Life); and
4. The ethos of research in and about writing across the curriculum that we promote through our center.

These four goals consequently guide the collaborations we seek and the partnerships to which we say yes.

These goals do not require long-term commitments, nor do they hinder them; consequently, the opportunity for growth is always present and the rewards of short-term projects are present as well. Many of the potential partners who come to us are exploring their options, so we do not want to scare them away by requiring long-term commitments, or by suggesting ambitious plans that may overwhelm them. Starting small allows both of us to invest relatively small amounts of staff time, energy, and even money as we figure out what works, what doesn't, what the perceived needs are, what the real needs are, and how we can both benefit from working together. Starting small usually means we can test the possibilities and weigh the options in a more timely fashion as well. Large projects must be written into budgets that are planned a year or more in advance, and often require a greater level of commitment and approval outside of the center or program. Often, small projects can be worked in more easily and may then provide useful data if we both decide to pursue a larger project down the road, with each other or with other interested partners.

A SAMPLING OF SHORT-TERM PARTNERSHIPS

To illustrate what I am promoting, I would like to start by describing a series of brief collaborations between our WAC-based university writing center and partners in local and alumni high schools, as well as with community organizations. I hope these descriptions of real collaborations will showcase the possibilities and help illuminate the value of such investments.

Working with High Schools

One common area of collaboration has been with new high school writing centers at both the planning stages and the start-up or fledgling stages. These collaborations may be as easy as an email conversation. Former students, writing center alumni, even university alumni who know we have a writing center at MSU often email and ask for help. They need resources, they want advice, they want to be able to say they can get support, even if it's just consultations, from the university. I have a folder of materials I share with them: proposals used for other high school centers, letters to principals, teachers, and parents, sample surveys, bibliographies, and course syllabi (see Chapter 6, McMullen-Light, for more about such sharing of materials). I also get them hooked into the network of other secondary writing centers and/or WCenter; if working with an alum who isn't local, I try to put this new director in contact with a writing center director in the area where the new center will be. Sometimes these materials and email conversations are all they need or want. If they are somewhat local, however, a visit is often the next step. A conversation in their space helps show our investment and usually prompts more specific questions about logistics and local context. Sometimes this investment leads to other collaborations, and sometimes it ends with the visit, and you have to be okay with it ending at this nebulous spot. You may not ever see the new writing center; you just know that you have done your best to help a new center or director get started and have served your colleagues and community.

Another type of short-term investment may be a bit more hands-on. Recently, for example, two local high schools started writing centers. They had a class and a center in operation before they fully figured out what they wanted to do or how they wanted to do it, so they called our center for help. A number of writing consultants on my staff were happy to go out to the schools and meet with the writing center consultants there. We were able to talk about some basic writing center concepts, such as the difference between revising and editing, helping students understand assignment sheets, working with writers from across the curriculum, when to say no to clients, and how to ask generative questions. We then hosted an open question and answer session that was successful for both of us. The high school students were able to voice some concerns, many of which they hadn't felt free to share with their advisor, while my consultants, many of whom hope to work with or start high school writing centers, learned some important caveats about operating in different types of spaces and contexts. We also invited these consultants to come visit our center at any time—to observe, to be a part of an event, and to have their own consultations. After the first visit, we tentatively planned to return to these schools in the next year and to host sessions for the staff at our center as a way to model consultations and to maintain this small collaboration. We have already had our first applicant from one of these students who is headed to our university for her freshman year. The authors of Chapter 8 describe such a mutually beneficial exchange, demonstrating the usefulness of understanding the contexts, roles, and experiences on either side of the partnership, and of making both partners responsible for the collaboration. We have returned to the schools and have had the same kinds of discussions and question/answer sessions with the new staff, but we have not been able to work out visits to campus or our writing center—yet, but we're still hopeful (and patient).

Patience can be important if your hope is to turn a short-term partnership into something more substantial, or into other short-term events. A few years ago, for example, Laurel, one of my former graduate student administrators from another writing center, contacted me. Laurel is now teaching high school outside of Washington, DC, and her school was starting a writing center. She stumbled upon a meeting one summer before the center was set to open and overheard some plans for the new center. Based on her writing center experience and study, Laurel was doubtful that their plan would work. After she interrupted the meeting and spoke up, she found herself the new co-director of the center with a colleague who had no writing center experience, but who was very excited about the prospects. Laurel called me to chat about their revised plans and to brainstorm some possibilities. Over the next year or so, we had a series of conversations about their new center and how the tutors and the program were progressing. When I found myself headed to an IWCA conference just an hour down the road from Laurel, she invited me to come visit her center and meet with her students. I was able to see her center in action, host a robust question and answer session with her tutors, and visit with some of her English classes. I continue to receive updates from Laurel, and I make sure I send relevant resources her way. I've also introduced her to some of the new high school writing center directors in my area (and on one occasion, an alum in her area), and she has continued to send me updates on their progress.

However, high school writing centers aren't the only way to serve area schools. We have also had short-term partnerships with a variety of college prep and student enrichment programs in the area. One summer, we worked specifically with the high school students in the Upward Bound program. Through collaboration with their language arts teacher, we offered a series of workshops on academic writing and research, peer review, and creative writing. Writing consultants then worked with a small team of students who had volunteered to be the editors of an anthology they were creating from the participants' work. Consultants guided them through the selection and editing processes, as well as the layout processes. With some financial help from our college dean, we then printed the anthologies for them—enough for students, parents, and representatives from their home schools and school system. The anthologies were distributed at a special celebratory event that included an open mic reading of some of the pieces, congratulations from a handful of local school officials, and a reception.

Spending an afternoon or two visiting a school or consulting with students at a local library is another way of investing with local students and schools that requires minimal preparation and commitment on either end. The main task is setting up a mutually viable date and recruiting volunteers to travel to the location in need (note, that you may also need to help student volunteers arrange carpools or figure out how a bus will get them to where they need to go). For example, over the past few years, we have been invited by a variety of teachers and programs to visit their schools and classrooms to consult with students on resumes and personal statements for college applications. Conversations about their writing also lead to discussions about college choices, choosing majors, what to expect when one gets to college, and other worries high school students have. These interactions help alleviate fears and make the high school-college transition easier. A similar endeavor included joining an existing collaboration between our professional writing program and a local elementary school to help them produce videos of stories they had written. The elementary students created the props needed for putting the story on film, shot the video, then worked with the college students to edit the film, including adding sound effects and voiceovers. When the film was complete, we were able to host a showcase night for the video's premiere and a display of the artwork/props used in this science fiction movie. On another day, we joined students from the MSU Poetry Center to consult with local students on poetry writing. These various short-term partnerships take our students into the schools, and also bring students and their families to the university, building good will on both sides and contributing to the overall community.

Working with/in the Community

Certainly our schools are a part of our community, but it is also possible to partner with the community in other ways. For example, we have sponsored music literacy retreats for several years. These retreats happen once or twice a year as the members of a local women's community chorus utilize our space to dissect the music they are singing that season. They use the technology of our center to have multimedia presentations on the composers and lyricists of the music being sung, as well as historical or cultural information relevant to the piece or genre. They brainstorm, write, discuss, and share as their way of understanding the music, so they can put those interpretations into what they sing. It began as a one-time event, because they needed an accessible space with the right equipment, but it has continued for several years. What has come from this is a growing archive of chorus materials and my own personal oral history research project, Voices of Sistrum, about the more than twenty-five year history of this organization and its role in the local gay and lesbian and women's communities.

A similar investment has our center going into the local public library once a week to sponsor a community creative writing group. Here, local writers gather each week—with a lot of variation in attendance—to write, to read, and to give feedback. Participants write poetry, short stories, creative non-fiction, and memoir. A couple of members are even working on novels that they share in pieces week to week. A couple of our consultants attend each week as facilitators and members, and serve as liaisons between our center and the library. Numerous events are growing from this small investment. The members of this group became the core of a writing marathon we hosted this past year, and they plan to host it again next year. They are also producing an anthology of the work written by participants, and twice a year, they come to campus to share their work with a wider audience at our open mic nights, which are scheduled once a semester. Also as a result of this small partnership, the library has begun discussions about us facilitating other workshops for library patrons: resume and cover letter writing, college application help, public speaking—all are topics community members have requested. Similarly, a couple of other libraries in the area have also asked to set up writing groups. Our next group will meet once a week after school at a different library, where area middle and high school students will receive writing consultations with their homework assignments from across the curriculum, as well as language help as needed for the many non-native speakers of English who frequent this library.

Our center also has an entire committee that has grown out of requests from community organizations for workshops on grant writing. Both groups and individuals have asked for help in researching and writing grants and for training their members to help with the grant writing process. Our first response was to create a grant writing workshop that was then given for the first group who asked for this help. When the workshop was requested again, consultants began revising the existing workshop and seeking help from experts across campus. From this endeavor, the grant writing committee grew, which is a popular committee for consultants who want to put to use the knowledge they gained in a departmental grant writing course, for those who want to learn more about grant writing, and for those who think grant writing skills are important for their career goals. This committee is now creating a series of videocasts about various aspects of grant writing through interviews with experts in our area both on and off campus. These videocasts will be available to the community and will more than likely spark additional requests for workshops and partnerships (both large and small).

Working across Electronic Spaces

As was mentioned previously, some short-term collaborations are about email support and discussions. Online chat features, blogs, and discussion boards can also be used to facilitate more in-depth conversations with groups of students, consultants, and community members. One semester, for example, we hosted a communal blog that was created to facilitate dialogue between our consultants in training, and new consultants, who were still in training at a writing center in Sweden. The two groups read some of the same assigned readings and were then able to respond to the readings and to each other online—broadening the discussion and allowing the two groups to see the different contexts that were influencing how students read the advice of writing center professionals. This partnership required a series of email conversations before both of our semesters started, agreement on a few mutual readings to assign students, and organization of the electronic platform for the exchange. Likewise, when a colleague from across the country asked for consultants to mentor her new high school writing consultants, I recruited several members of my staff to serve as their online buddies. A simple call for volunteers on our staff listserv yielded more partners than we actually needed. Those who were assigned buddies reported email conversations about readings, sharing consulting stories, answering questions about sessions as well as college in general, and making new friends.

Whether it's an online conversation, a revision workshop in the local library, or a training session at the high school down the road, these short-term collaborations have been important to those involved. My consultants enjoy the opportunities to have experiences with writers outside of our center; they also feel encouraged by the investment they see from other readers and writers in the community and in the schools. Students we have worked with have emailed to say thanks, and to suggest further programming. At orientation just this summer, a student who was not a tutor but who saw us on her campus, stopped by our information table to say, "You came to our school. I'll come check you out this fall." As a bonus, our college likes to brag about our partnerships, and counts our ventures into the schools and communities in their annual outreach figures. These low-risk, short-term collaborations have built a great deal of good will, and have certainly been worth our center's time and attention.

FROM SHORT-TERM TO LONG-TERM PARTNERSHIPS: A CASE STUDY

One partnership that started out small and has continued to grow is a hybrid of many of the forms discussed above: Grandparents University. I'd like to use Grandparents University as a case study to further illustrate how short-term collaborations can help you meet your institutional goals, enrich your consultants' experiences, and evolve into something bigger and more permanent.

Grandparents University is a program sponsored by a collaborative of alumni organizations from across our university. For three days, pairs of grandparents and grandchildren live on campus, stay in the dorms, eat in the cafeterias, and attend workshops designed specifically for them. These workshops are intended to highlight all of the various areas of interest across campus and to be hands-on for the participants. During registration, participants indicate their top preferences and then attend approximately four classes as a pair (out of more than fifty offerings from across the curriculum), as well as evening activities for the whole cohort. When the program began in 2006, the writing center offered one workshop on digital storytelling. The participant pairs came in, discussed storytelling and video making, created a storyboard for the brief story they wanted to tell, then filmed or took pictures in order to tell their story. They then worked on our center computers in iMovie to create and edit their videos; consultants were around to help at every stage, but most importantly at the last drafting and editing stage. After Grandparents University was over, consultants completed some final editing of these projects, then participants were mailed copies of their movie on DVD.

The success of this first small partnership then began to grow in both scope and size, and has increased in some way each of the past seven years. As a whole, the Grandparents University program has been successful and has expanded each year, and we have done our part to support and add to this growth. The digital storytelling workshop, for example, has grown into a two-part workshop that happens on two different days, with extended time for each part. This format gives the participants more time to plan and get consultant help with brainstorming and storyboard drafting, then time away from us and across the university to take still and video pictures for their movies. On the second day, they have more time for drafting and editing, including their voice-overs and music; they can then leave with their movie burned to DVD or a jump drive that day—no waiting for a DVD in the mail. In addition, the writing center has added two more workshops to this partnership—one that asks participants to think about the genre of the comic book, and then teaches them how to make their own in the program Comic Life. They then create their own comic stories or scrapbooks during a two-part workshop. In addition, we offer a memoir writing workshop that gets participants started in drafting a life narrative or creative non-fiction piece, and also encourages them to keep a journal of ideas for future writing projects. All of our workshops are well attended and receive positive feedback. But the partnership hasn't stopped there.

Grandparents University reaches a wide number of MSU alumni and community members. As a result, we have had area teachers contact us about doing some of these same workshops for their students. For example, one teacher has brought in two different fifth-grade classes for the Comic Life workshop. Working with composers at different educational and developmental levels has been good for our consultants, helping them stay sharp and truly focused on the needs of their clients in a specific moment. In addition, a number of research projects have grown from our work with Grandparents University. It was a research project that led to the initial expansion of the workshop, for example. Another round of assessment conducted by our facilitators, as they prepared for a conference presentation and utilized participant surveys, led to using two different days for the program, and made sure our participants could leave with their final products. Also, a consultant was interested in how participants' attitudes about technology might change as they went through the workshop, especially the attitudes of the grandparents, who often demonstrated some fear of the technology. A series of pre- and post-attitudinal surveys were used to investigate this research question, and the participants were happy to be involved in such a research project. Because the project is short-term at only three days each year, but is also ongoing with a variety of different participants, it has become a perfect venue for consultants to develop and hone their skills in the areas of research and assessment, making them better students, researchers, and consultants.

RECOMMENDATIONS FOR BUILDING YOUR OWN SHORT-TERM WAC COLLABORATIONS

- **Be open and listen.** Possibilities for partnerships can arise in a wide variety of ways: A conversation at a committee meeting, over lunch, or in the grocery store; a request through our center email or my own personal email account; or a suggestion from a client or consultant. My strategy is to listen specifically for ways our center can intervene or serve. Can we provide a space? Do you need some volunteers? Do you need a workshop that we can provide? More often than not, I try to find a way to say yes that doesn't overly commit us in terms of personnel, time, or money at the beginning of the partnership, because we can always extend and expand at a later date.

- **Do your research**. What are the needs in your community? Attend community events and find out. Attend workshops and committee meetings that are about partnerships, especially events that may feature potential community partners. Invite community members to your events so they can see what you're doing and think about how they could be part of it. Our community creative writing groups grew from a focus group we sponsored with area literacy leaders as we investigated ways to be more involved with our immediate geographic area.
- **Talk about what you're doing**. Word of mouth is one of the best ways to develop new partners. Talking about a partnership with one group may spark ideas with another group. Letting your colleagues across campus and in the community know the breadth and variety of your work will help them think about you when they need the kinds of expertise your center or program has to offer. We are often called upon by other units on campus to provide one event, one workshop, or one day of services as part of a lengthier program that is occurring over time on campus.
- **Advertise what you're doing**. If you have a website, a Facebook page, a Twitter account, or other social media accounts, use them to advertise your partnerships and programming. This again will spark ideas for others, and may prompt potential partners to contact you. It will also prompt volunteers to get involved.
- **Record or count what you're doing**. Count the people you reach with your short-term collaborations, list these outreach contacts in your annual reports, and show how they benefit those involved, including the larger school community(ies). Most directors, whether tenured faculty, administrative staff, or some other label/title, have a charge for service work and possibly outreach or engagement. Count all of the times you consult with area teachers or visit local schools; those you report to will be happy to pass these positive statistics along the administrative line.
- **Play matchmaker**. Don't be afraid to say "no" or "not now." Sometimes, you aren't the best fit or the solution to a problem. However, if you know which program or person would be a better fit, make introductions and help them get started. The favor will more than likely be returned down the road.
- **Have fun**. Enjoyable, interesting partnerships and collaborations can be contagious and become a point of pride. They get people excited and usually lead to more projects (often bigger projects if that's what you desire); and on a pragmatic note, they can lead to more funding.

My argument here is simple: value the possibilities of short-term partnerships and collaborations. One-time events may be repeated and expand into larger events. Helping one high school may lead to discussions that send other high schools your way. A successful workshop with a community group may open up doors for other workshops and/or other groups. You never know where your short-term WAC collaborations may lead. However, don't be disappointed if the partnership stops with just the one workshop, the single event, or the isolated visit. These singular occasions have their value as well, and should be celebrated in their own right, acknowledging that you and your program are team players invested in your school and community.

CHAPTER 10

WHAT WE HAVE LEARNED ABOUT WAC PARTNERSHIPS AND THEIR FUTURES

Jacob S. Blumner and Pamela B. Childers

In 1992, Pam wrote an article for *Writing Lab Newsletter* on writing center collaborations entitled "College/High School Connections" in which she described both the problems and advantages of high school-college writing center collaborations. She saw the problems as a "lack of mutual understanding of roles as educators, time restraints, pre-established roles of participants, pecking order hierarchy, and why get involved with another institution" (Farrell 1). The advantages of partnerships were seen as "interactive training of tutors, exchange of ideas to survive the politics of education, focus on clear goals, shared expenses, and intellectual development" (Farrell 5). Over two decades later, little has changed.

After years of work with WAC partnerships, including the individual data gathered by our colleagues in their chapters of this book, we have learned more than we had imagined. First, there are many commonalities described in these chapters that reinforce the results of our original survey for our 2011 article in the *WAC Journal*. They include:

- Respectful, collaborative nature of partnership
- Jointly initiated collaborations
- Involvement of many stakeholders in development to benefit all
- Integration of programs into the fabric of all institutions involved
- Importance of information sharing (transparency)
- All or part of funding provided by both institutions
- Partnerships formed around local contexts
- Involvement of teacher preparation and faculty development
- Involvement of students through variations of a writing center or writing fellows program

These responses are unsurprising, yet they provide more evidence for the kinds of conditions required for successful partnerships, no matter the context, size, number of partners, or resources. These are not rules, but they do repeatedly resurface in our research. When asked about his research of dual credit courses for his dissertation, James Uhlenkamp, Director of Field Experience, Gleazer School of Education at Graceland University, responded:

> The success largely depends on the college offering a predictable set of classes at a time when the HS schedule can accommodate them; on the HS providing a teacher willing and able to deliver a class at the college level, including at the college pace, which tends to be much more intense than the HS classes; and on the two entities having a solid and understandable contract governing the expenses, expectations, responsibilities, and opportunities the partnership affords.

In contrast, we also see what most of our authors, as well as respondents to surveys and interviews, describe as the "uniqueness of every partnership." Therefore, many of the commonalities have been listed in more general terms to fit those individual partnerships, while each collaboration has some little quirks that make it different from any other one. For instance, many of Trixie Smith's short-term partnerships have specific qualities that are dependent upon the institutions or community groups involved. And, even though we hate to admit it, most of the partnerships we have located involve English/writing teachers and some science or history partnerships. In the undercurrent of these partnerships are hidden ones involving mathematics, art, music, physical education and foreign language classes. They may begin when two educators meet at a conference and decide to try an online exchange involving secondary education majors and a high school music, art, mathematics or foreign language class. Deborah Snider of Southern Utah University is editing a special issue of *The Clearing House* (2016) called "Drawing from Within: The Arts & Animated Learning" that will include secondary-college partnerships on writing in art. And, we are hearing about more projects in future articles on a social science-mathematics partnership that involves WAC, another based on research into the value of using English-speaking music (especially lyrics) to teach English to students in China, and yet another discussing the value of teaching writing across disciplines in high school for successful writing in college history classes. So, the importance of WAC continues to go beyond our limited work here.

In the spring of 2014 we wanted to gather more perspectives on WAC partnerships, so we invited international educators from California to Germany in secondary, community college, and university writing programs to respond to another survey. Based on their anonymous responses, we noticed similar patterns to those mentioned above. However, we learned more specific information from their responses to the following questions:

1. If you have had experience with WAC partnerships through professional organizations or with colleagues or individuals at other institutions, describe a successful one. What made it work?
2. If you have had experience with a partnership that was less successful, what would you have done differently to improve the partnership?
3. As a professional educator, what do you predict about WAC partnerships in the future? What might/should they look like? Will they be needed?
4. What words of encouragement can you offer to present and future collaborators?

Responses to each of these questions brought similar ideas of what made the collaborations successful. Common responses to Question 1 included mutual respect, common goals, need for a clear plan with goals, faculty development and common scholarship, flexibility in communication, and dedication of teachers and administrators. A secondary educator appreciated "encouragement to pair up with a faculty member from another discipline and create an autonomous lesson that drew upon the expertise of the instructors to showcase another way of approaching their discipline." Respondents also mentioned attendance at conferences, such as CCCC and discipline-specific ones to bring back ideas for colleagues to implement, and use of the WAC Clearinghouse website (wac.colostate.edu) that offers many professional open-access books and journals as resources. One university respondent mentioned co-consulting with a secondary WAC specialist as an important part of a successful collaboration that impacted changes in curriculum and staff development, as well as collaborative presentations at conferences. Another respondent noted that mutual respect meant "going into the relationship knowing that you have a lot to learn from each other. It also means remembering that you are all concerned about the same thing: the students' success." One university respondent described her successful partnership as follows:

> While in the college setting, email is the expected means of communication for pretty much everything, my WAC partnership with secondary school teachers requires a lot of texting. It also requires that I occasionally just show up, in person, in the high school classroom (even if that means dropping in unexpectedly). Sometimes it means sending messages through liaisons, such as a college student who happens to be interning at the high school. All these "back channel" means of communication are necessary to make sure we're on the same page. Also necessary is getting to know one another outside of the school environment—by meeting for brunch, going out for drinks, hosting a cookout, etc.

But what problems did respondents encounter that they would handle differently? Mainly administrative issues, such as constant changes at the top in schools struggling to find stability, while new people come in "with goals of productivity not learning," overworking teachers. One respondent described how leaders of the partnership "insisted on a very formulaic way of writing the experience up that many found off-putting, and the project was paired (needlessly) with another effort to map the skills involved in particular courses." They speak of consultants brought in "to conduct a workshop but not build a relationship." In handling the situation differently, they mentioned that the WAC partnership should be "on the books" as a course or real project, and faculty in-house training enables all partners to have the same terminology and understanding for better communication.

In considering the future of WAC partnerships, most respondents had very clear individual concerns, so we will try to offer the most common suggestions. One university respondent emphasized that WAC at universities has "to grow organically, within departments and from individuals within departments.... we need to stop the one size fits all models that still prevail. WAC needs to transition to CxC or another name and engage in the five languages (visual, oral, alphabetical, mathematical, physical)." The majority of respondents clearly felt that the need for WAC partnerships would increase in the future because of revisions in the SAT and CCSS that include writing across disciplines, a resurgence in popularity of WAC due to an emphasis on literacy, the need for writing in job readiness, and advancements in writing in higher education and professional training that we cannot even predict. Several respondents offered valuable comments on this question. For instance, one respondent said:

> The testing agenda that drives many high school curricula (currently at least) does not have a clear analog at the college level, so it's hard for educators in the different contexts to truly see where each other is coming from. At the same time, that's exactly WHY we need these partnerships: because, if we want students to enter colleges with the habits of mind that colleges value, high school and college teachers (and administrators) need to be talking with one another. In addition, true partnerships between high school and college instructors help remind the college-level faculty that they can learn a lot from their K-12 counterparts.

While another respondent added, "I think that they [WAC partnerships] will become more numerous and necessary, if for no other reason than job readiness is becoming the coin of the realm. I think that the stand-alone English department that focuses primarily on literature is fading and that kind of 'English' will be folded into other programs while writing will become more distributed."

So, what do WAC educators say to current and future WAC collaborators? More than anything else, they emphasize that it should be a reciprocal relationship in which all involved are learners as well as teachers who are passionate about the partnership. They also suggest strong communication among members of the partnership—teachers, administrators, students—to eliminate misunderstandings. Also, they remind others that change takes time, so patience is required through the stressful times of beginning the partnership. Again, they mentioned the need for a contract or concrete document that outlines the goals of the partnership. In valuing one's colleagues in a partnership, a respondent noted, "there is a core of literacy-focused, imaginative teachers in our state whom we have been able to tap as inspiring speakers and workshop leaders." As one high school respondent said, "Working with a colleague from another discipline liberates me from the chains of my own ignorance. I became an educator, in part, because I loved to learn—not just English—and such partnerships create a natural bridge to new knowledge and experiences."

Finally, partnerships exist beyond the university with individual connections that begin in high school. For instance, Austin Lin, a high school student interested in writing across the disciplines through the writing center, changed his major from English to chemical engineering while at Johns Hopkins University. However, he continues to value writing in his current field by writing a blog for StayWithIt.org, a group started by the White House Council on Jobs and Competitiveness to reduce attrition from engineering programs for undergrads (http://staywithit.org/blog-entry/tennysons-daydream-what-engineering-majors-and-poets-have-common). In Austin's words, "I write about the importance that writing had in making me a better engineer—in my case, writing across the curriculum literally made me a better engineer" (Lin). Brandall Jones, recent college graduate, commented on his high school experiences that he now uses; "I agree that the collaboration between college professors and secondary school teachers is imperative, in order to adequately prepare students for college writing.... I find myself helping friends here with writing challenges that are a breeze for me" (Jones).

Perhaps the most prominent example of lifelong influence on partnerships may be Tommy Tobin, who worked with Pam and Trixie Smith through the Tennessee Writing Center Collaborative when he was in high school. While he attended Stanford, Tommy wrote an article for publication about the importance of high school preparation for college writing (Tobin) that he revised with assistance from Stanford's Andrea Lunsford (writing program director) and Clyde Moneyhun (writing center director), then he presented with high school students and Dilek Tokay of Sabanci University in Turkey at the 2007 WAC conference in Austin, Texas. Now, while completing a law degree at Georgetown and working on a Master's degree in public policy at Harvard's Kennedy School, Tommy presented on WAC partnerships at the 2014 European Writing Center Conference in Germany with authors Luise Beaumont (Chapter 7) and Kirsten Jamsen (Chapter 8). And, how many individual examples continue throughout the world? These are the hidden future of WAC partnerships; however, we can also make some more visible predictions based on what we have learned from others.

We see two ways in the short term that these partnerships will advance; the first is legislative and societal. More and more federal, state, and local governments are involving themselves in student success and education, and demands are increasing to prepare students for life after school. Part of that pressure is from stakeholders (students, parents, employers) questioning the bifurcation of K-12 to higher education. The legislative and societal pressure will demand increased accountability, and writing will be a key component of that because of its civic and professional importance. Arguably, as with many other educational movements that have arisen from legislative mandate, the vision may be limiting and highly focused on accountability.

Danielle Lilge in "Illuminating Possibilities: Secondary Writing Across the Curriculum as a Resource for Navigating Common Core State Standards" describes ways in which secondary school teachers can apply writing in classrooms across disciplines with the help of WAC advocates (college and university colleagues in all disciplines). She concludes, "WAC suggests the possibility for reconceptualizing CCSS-driven writing instruction in secondary classrooms not as addendum but rather as central to content area learning—a necessary support in meaning making and understanding." Lilge argues that the connection between WAC and the CCSS movement is an obvious one where these WAC advocates can make a difference at the secondary level.

The second way we see WAC partnerships advancing is through educators seeing the value of the work for students, producing results and scholarship about the work, and convincing school administrations that this work should be valued and supported. With the heavy push toward civic engagement of our colleges and universities and the growing need for support of our secondary schools, WAC partnerships provide an avenue to benefit all involved. Professional organizations, such as the Coalition of Urban and Metropolitan Universities, see civic engagement by higher education as a moral imperative, and literacy partnerships are often a central component of that engagement. As more partnerships are formed and shared, others will be able to replicate and improve on the models. Then, ideally, this informed work will be used to educate communities and legislative bodies, which can in turn further promote and support this important work.

If one were to think like a futurist, one might imagine an educational system that completely breaks down the barriers of moving from the K-12 system to higher education. Sometimes we hear the term K-16 education, a nod to seeing education as a continuum without a vast chasm between twelfth grade and college. Some form of higher education is becoming essential for professional success, and the benefits to personal growth are also well documented. WAC partnerships can lead the way to a seamless education that moves beyond the nineteenth century model of education to something that better serves our students in the twenty-first century.

Although robots are already writing for humans (Thompson 2014), we also predict that the collaborative efforts of educators will be necessary to prepare others to record research and advancements across disciplines. Today, much of what we do is not read by the masses, but it will still be necessary to advance society globally. Though nefarious, programmers have developed computer programs to create "gobblygook" academic conference proposals and academic papers (Thompson), pushing us closer to computer-generated content. According to the *New York Times*, computer-generated newspaper articles are gaining traction in the newsroom (Lohr 2011). What will be the role of writers in the future? Educators can and should play a role in that future, and that role can be stronger if educators are in partnership across the borders of K-12 and higher education.

From individual short-term partnerships, as Trixie Smith describes in Chapter 9, to cross-institutional collaborations, communication across disciplines will continue to support cultural advancements and service to others. Because university and secondary schools may become something totally different from what they are today, we will also see new ways that we can partner globally. Skype, Apple's Siri, and other technologies are just the beginning of what we may expect and learn from the advancements of WAC collaborators in other countries. As long as there is the need for shared information across disciplines, there will be a need for WAC partnerships.

Based on the survey responses and the valuable insights our authors have brought to this book, we truly believe that WAC partnerships, no matter what we call them, will become even more important to us as educators and to our students at all academic levels in preparing them for the next phases of their lives.

WORKS CITED

Blumner, Jacob, and Pamela Childers. "Building Better Bridges: What Makes High School-College WAC Collaborations Work?" *The WAC Journal* 22 (2011): 91-101. Web. 1 Nov. 2014.

Farrell, Pamela. "College/High School Connections." *Writing Lab Newsletter* 16.1 (May-June 1992): 1+. Web.

Jones, Brandall. "Poetry and Readings." Message to Pamela Childers. 13 January 2013. Email.

Lilge, Danielle. "Illuminating Possibilities: Secondary Writing Across the Curriculum as a Resource for Navigating Common Core State Standards." Across the Disciplines 9.3 (2012): n. pag. Web. 25 July 2013.

Lin, Austin. "Poetry, Chemical Engineering and Career Advancement." Message to Pamela Childers. 1 April 2014. Email.

Lohr, Steve. "In Case You Wondered, a Real Human Wrote This Column." *New York Times*. 11 Sept. 2011. Web. 3 Nov. 2014.

Thompson, Clive. "How to Tell When a Robot Has Written You a Letter: The Next Turing Test? Handwriting." *The Message*. 23 Sept. 2014. Web. 24 Sept. 2014.<https://medium.com/message/how-to-tell-when-a-robot-has-written-you-a-letter-701562705d59>.

Tobin, Tommy. "The Writing Center as a Key Actor in Secondary School Preparation." *The Clearing House* 83.6 (2010): 230-34.

Uhlenkamp, James. "RE: Thanks." Message to Pamela Childers. 21 June 2014. Email.

Uhlenkamp, J. J. (2012). "Do credit-based transfer programs have an impact on intellectual development from secondary education to post-secondary education?" Diss. The University of Nebraska-Lincoln, 2012. Web.

CONTRIBUTORS

Luise Beaumont is a Writing Program and Writing Center enthusiast. She is coordinator of the Writing Center at New York University Abu Dhabi where she is planning on conducting research for her PhD. Luise is particularly interested in tutor training, multilingualism in the Writing Center and integrating creative writing methods in tutoring undergraduate students. She has co-authored multiple articles and chapters as well as presented on WAC, Writing Center practices and creative writing strategies.

Jacob S. Blumner is Director of the Marian E. Wright Writing Center and Associate Professor of English at the University of Michigan-Flint. He has co-edited two books, and his work has appeared in *The WAC Journal*, *Across the Disciplines*, and *Praxis: A Writing Center Journal*. He lives at home with his wife, three sons, and an overweight orange cat.

Malcolm Graeme Childers is a former college art professor who chose to devote his time to creating visual art, music and creative writing. Besides producing a collection of relief etchings that are part of his multi-media book, *Roadsongs: A Journey into the Life and Mindscape of an American Artist*, he has also produced the Rocky Mountain PBS documentary *Roadsongs: A Journey into the Rocky Mountain West*. His interest in Writing Across the Curriculum includes giving workshops and presentations at major professional conferences on writing, writing centers, and English.

Pamela B. Childers, Caldwell Chair of Composition Emerita at McCallie School, is Executive Editor of *The Clearing House*. Recipient of the IWCA Outstanding Service Award, she serves on WAC and writing center boards and has written numerous articles, chapters, *The High School Writing Center*, *Programs and Practices: Writing Across the Secondary School* (with Gere and Young), and *ARTiculating: Teaching Writing in a Visual World* (with Hobson and Mullin). Pam consults on writing with all academic levels.

Michelle Cox, founding director of Bridgewater State University's WAC program, is Director of the English Language Support Office at Cornell University, which provides support for international graduate students. She serves on *Across the Disciplines* and *WAC Clearinghouse* editorial boards, and on the International WAC Board of Consultants. She recently published (with co-editor Terry Myers Zawacki) *WAC and Second Language Writers: Research toward Linguistically and Culturally Inclusive Programs and Practices* (WAC Clearinghouse/Parlor Press, 2014).

Contributors

Phyllis Gimbel is Associate Professor, Educational Leadership at Bridgewater State University, where she served as the Assistant Coordinator of Writing Across the Curriculum and Faculty Fellow in the Office of Teaching and Learning. Phyllis has published and presented on school leadership and on faculty development. Her second book, *Healthy Schools: The Hidden Component of Teaching and Learning,* was published in October 2013. Phyllis received the V. James DiNardo Alumni Award for Excellence in Teaching at Bridgewater State University.

Marie Hansen is an English Language Arts teacher at Burnsville High School, where she teaches eleventh-grade English, leads their writing center, and directs student theater productions. Marie is also a teacher consultant for the Minnesota Writing Project, an active member of the E12 Writing Centers Collective, and a graduate student at the University of St. Thomas in the masters in literature program. In 2011, she received the Minnesota Council of Teachers of English Developing Leadership Award for her passion and enthusiasm in the field.

Debra Hartley is a co-director and webmaster of the Center for Writing at the University of Minnesota-Twin Cities, co-coordinator of Student Writing Support, and technology liaison for the Minnesota Writing Project. She belongs to Writing Center Professionals of Minnesota and the E12 Writing Centers Collective. Her professional interests include the use of technology in writing centers and classrooms and digital storytelling.

Kirsten Jamsen is the director of the Center for Writing at the University of Minnesota-Twin Cities and co-director of the Minnesota Writing Project. She is active in many national and regional professional organizations, and co-founded the Writing Center Professionals of Minnesota and the E12 Writing Centers Collective. With her colleagues, she studies writing consultancy, writing across the curriculum, teacher professional development, and the role of technology in writing centers and classrooms.

Katie Levin is a co-directorof the Center for Writing at the University of Minnesota-Twin Cities, where she co-coordinates Student Writing Support and leads the Center's Interdisciplinary Studies of Writing program. A member of many national and regional professional associations, she is new to high school writing centers and is grateful for her E12 Writing Centers Collective colleagues' knowledge and experience. She focuses on the push-and-pull of power, discourse, identity, and resistance in and through writing centers.

Michael J. Lowry is a science teacher at the McCallie School in Chattanooga, TN. A member of the National Science Teachers Association (NSTA), he most recently served as its High School Division Director. He is Nationally Board Certified (physics) and a Presidential Awardee for Excellence in Science Teaching, and frequently leads workshops and writes about how writing may be used to enhance teaching and learning in science. Michael has also received

NEH, NOAA and NASA fellowships.

Michael McClellan holds a bachelor of science in chemistry from UW-La-Crosse, plus a master in teaching and a master in education administration from National-Louis University. He currently teaches at Forreston High School in Illinois. He became a chemistry/physical science teacher at Jefferson High School in Rockford, IL in 2005-2006 where he taught for seven years. He has coached varsity baseball and basketball for twenty years. He also has taught graduate communications and leadership courses at National-Louis University for four years.

Mary McMullen-Light directed the WAC Program at MCC-Longview for over twenty years, collaborating with faculty in general education, career and technical programs. She serves on the Board of Consultants for the International WAC Network and contributed to the Statement of WAC Principles and Practices. She has presented at the International WAC Conference and CCCC. Mary has worked at an alternative high school and is Research Coordinator for Outcomes Assessment at Johnson County Community College.

Dawn Myelle-Watson teaches sections of biology and physical science for honors, "mainstream," and at-risk students in Jefferson High School in Rockford, IL, where she also serves as the Freshman Academy Coordinator.

Federico Navarro is a professor and researcher at Universidad de Buenos Aires, Universidad Nacional de General Sarmiento and CONICET (Argentina). He is the Colegio de la Ciudad Writing Program coordinator. His research interests include genre pedagogy and professional communication. He has co-authored "Escribir para aprender" (2013), edited "Manual de escritura para carreras de humanidades" (in press) and published in Boletín de Filología, RMIE, Bellaterra, Nebrija, Páginas de Guarda and Texturas.

Kristen Nichols-Besel recently completed her PhD in the Department of Curriculum and Instruction at the University of Minnesota-Twin Cities, where she consulted with undergraduate and graduate writers at the University's Center for Writing. Prior to graduate school, she taught high school English language arts in Iowa. Currently, she teaches pre-service teachers at the College of St. Scholastica and works in the writing center at Bethel University. Her research interests include young adult literature and engagement of adolescents.

Brad Peters is Professor of English, coordinator of WAC, and director of undergraduate studies in English at Northern Illinois University. He prepares teacher-licensure candidates in writing instruction and teaches graduate courses in rhetoric. With Joonna Trapp, he co-edits the *Journal of the Assembly for Advanced Perspective in Learning* (JAEPL).

Mandy Pydde completed training as Peer Tutor in Writing while doing her studies in intercultural communication (M.A.). She worked as peer tutor in writing for two years at the Writing Center of the European University (Frankfurt

Oder/Germany). Mandy Pydde was part of a team that aimed at establishing WAC and peer tutoring in writing at German high schools. She also held numerous writing workshops for university students, high school students and teachers.

Andrea Revel Chion is a teacher of biology and health at secondary schools and a lecturer of biology didactics at teacher training colleges. She is also a professor and researcher at the University of Buenos Aires. Her publications include textbooks and several papers in educational journals. She is the co-author of "Escribir para aprender" (2013). Her research focuses on school scientific argumentation in relation to health and on narratives as a learning tool.

Trixie G. Smith is director of The Writing Center at Michigan State University. Her memberships include IWAC, IWCA, ECWCA, CCCC, MiWCA, and NWSA; she presently serves on the boards of both IWCA and ECWCA. Her publications include textbooks on WAC/WID and FYW and articles/chapters on writing centers, mentoring, and gender. Trixie's current research focuses on working with graduate and faculty writers; queer mentoring and pedagogy; and an oral history project about Sistrum, Lansing Women's Chorus.

Debora Spears is Literacy Leader at Jefferson High School. She has a master's degree in special education from the University of Illinois, a master in curriculum instruction from National Louis University, and a master in reading from Rockford University. Seven of her twenty-one years in teaching were spent working with disabled pre-schoolers. She has co-taught professional development courses in writing across the curriculum for six years.

Simone Tschirpke is part of academic staff at the Writing Center of the Europa Universität Viadrina, Frankfurt (Oder) Germany. She is involved in everyday writing center work and in peer tutor education. Together with collegues Simone founded the journal JoSch—Journal der Schreibberatung which is especially supporting peer tutors to publish their perspectives and experiences.

David Wellen of Jefferson High School teaches the full range of honors, mainstream, and at-risk students in his biology classes. He specializes in working with students who struggle to complete their required course credits in biology. He has also coached football and wrestling for many years.

Art Young is Robert S. Campbell Chair and Professor of English Emeritus at Clemson University, where he founded and coordinated Clemson's award-winning communication-across-the-curriculum program (1990-2009). In March 2002, Art received the Exemplar Award from the Conference on College Composition and Communication for outstanding achievement in teaching, research, and service. He has published extensively on Writing Across the Curriculum and in other areas connected to the theory and teaching of writing.

www.ingramcontent.com/pod-product-compliance
Lightning Source LLC
Chambersburg PA
CBHW032215230426
43672CB00011B/2561